REBELS RESURGENT
Fredericksburg to Chancellorsville

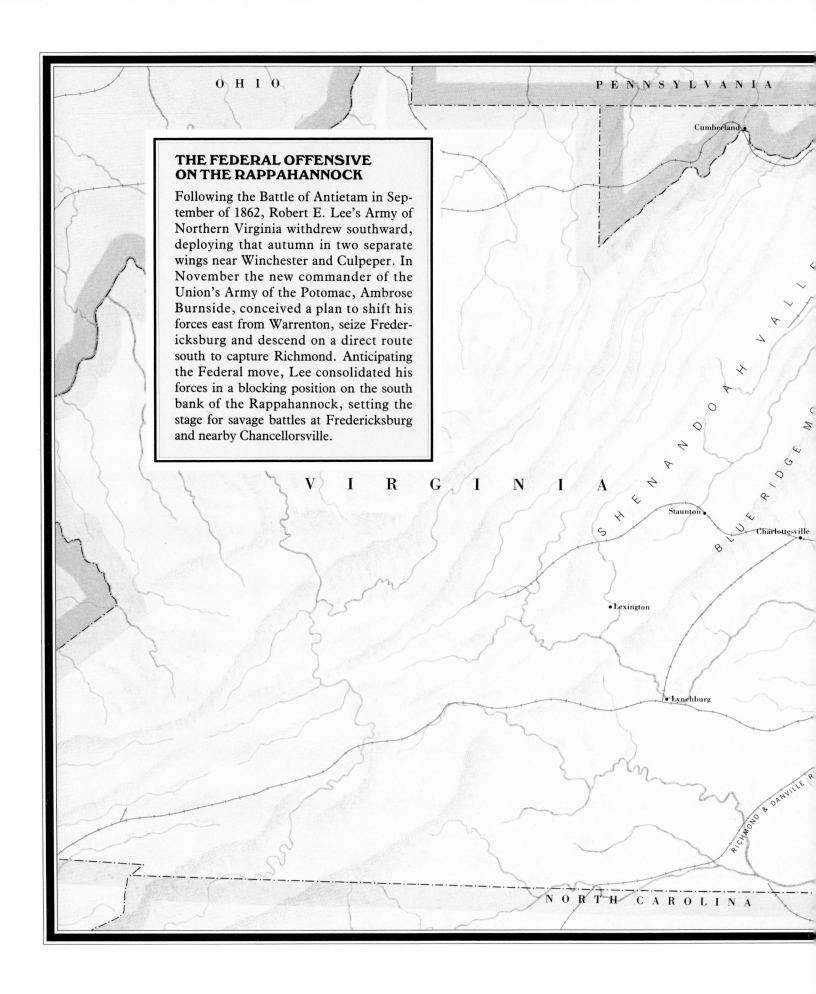

THE FEDERAL OFFENSIVE ON THE RAPPAHANNOCK

Following the Battle of Antietam in September of 1862, Robert E. Lee's Army of Northern Virginia withdrew southward, deploying that autumn in two separate wings near Winchester and Culpeper. In November the new commander of the Union's Army of the Potomac, Ambrose Burnside, conceived a plan to shift his forces east from Warrenton, seize Fredericksburg and descend on a direct route south to capture Richmond. Anticipating the Federal move, Lee consolidated his forces in a blocking position on the south bank of the Rappahannock, setting the stage for savage battles at Fredericksburg and nearby Chancellorsville.

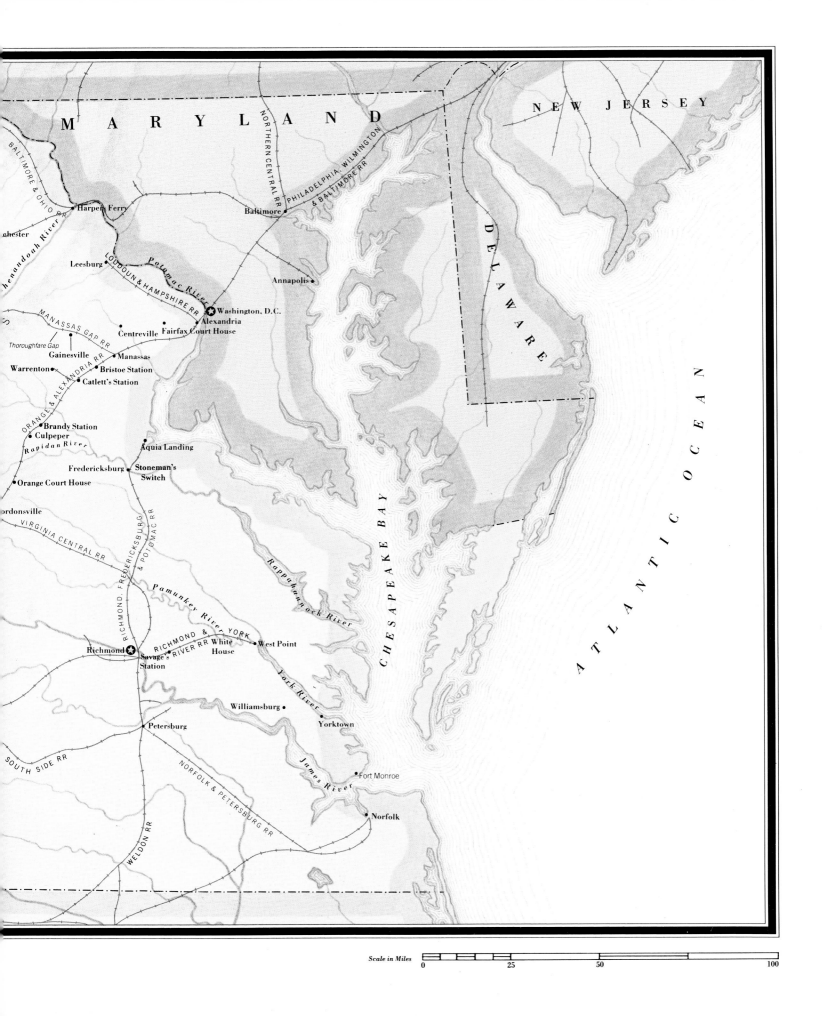

NEW JERSEY

MARYLAND

DELAWARE

ATLANTIC OCEAN

CHESAPEAKE BAY

BALTIMORE & OHIO RR

Harpers Ferry

chester

Shenandoah River

Leesburg

LOUDOUN & HAMPSHIRE RR

Potomac River

Baltimore

NORTHERN CENTRAL RR

PHILADELPHIA, WILMINGTON & BALTIMORE RR

Annapolis

Washington, D.C.

Alexandria

Fairfax Court House

Centreville

MANASSAS GAP RR

Thoroughfare Gap

Gainesville

Manassas

ORANGE & ALEXANDRIA RR

Warrenton

Bristoe Station

Catlett's Station

Brandy Station

Culpeper

Rapidan River

Aquia Landing

Fredericksburg

Stoneman's Switch

Orange Court House

ordonsville

VIRGINIA CENTRAL RR

RICHMOND, FREDERICKSBURG & POTOMAC RR

Pamunkey River

YORK RIVER RR

RICHMOND & YORK

White House

West Point

Richmond

Savage's Station

York River

Williamsburg

Yorktown

Rappahannock River

Petersburg

SOUTH SIDE RR

NORFOLK & PETERSBURG RR

James River

Fort Monroe

Norfolk

WELDON RR

Scale in Miles

0   25   50   100

TIME
LIFE
BOOKS

Other Publications:

YOUR HOME
THE ENCHANTED WORLD
THE KODAK LIBRARY OF CREATIVE PHOTOGRAPHY
GREAT MEALS IN MINUTES
PLANET EARTH
COLLECTOR'S LIBRARY OF THE CIVIL WAR
THE EPIC OF FLIGHT
THE GOOD COOK
THE SEAFARERS
WORLD WAR II
HOME REPAIR AND IMPROVEMENT
THE OLD WEST

For information on and a full description of any of the
Time-Life Books series listed above, please write:
Reader Information, Time-Life Books
541 North Fairbanks Court, Chicago, Illinois 60611

This volume is one of a series that chronicles in full the
events of the American Civil War, 1861-1865.
Other books in the series include:
Brother against Brother: The War Begins
First Blood: Fort Sumter to Bull Run
The Blockade: Runners and Raiders
The Road to Shiloh: Early Battles in the West
Forward to Richmond: McClellan's Peninsular Campaign
Decoying the Yanks: Jackson's Valley Campaign
Confederate Ordeal: The Southern Home Front
Lee Takes Command: From Seven Days to Second Bull Run
The Coastal War: Chesapeake Bay to Rio Grande
Tenting Tonight: The Soldier's Life
The Bloodiest Day: The Battle of Antietam
War on the Mississippi: Grant's Vicksburg Campaign

The Cover: Generals Thomas J. "Stonewall"
Jackson *(left)* and Robert E. Lee meet near midday on May 1, 1863, to devise tactics against
the Federal advance near Chancellorsville. On
the following day Jackson led his troops on a
daring flank attack that turned a potential Confederate disaster into a brilliant victory.

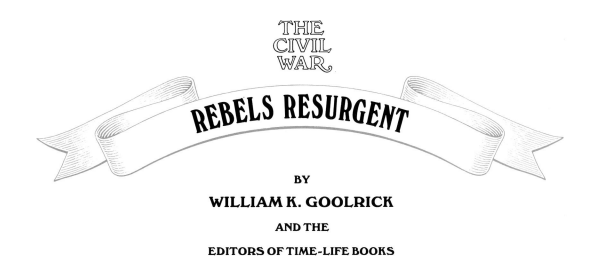

THE
CIVIL
WAR

REBELS RESURGENT

BY

WILLIAM K. GOOLRICK

AND THE

EDITORS OF TIME-LIFE BOOKS

Fredericksburg to Chancellorsville

TIME-LIFE BOOKS, ALEXANDRIA, VIRGINIA

Time-Life Books Inc.
is a wholly owned subsidiary of

TIME INCORPORATED

FOUNDER: Henry R. Luce 1898-1967

Editor-in-Chief: Henry Anatole Grunwald
President: J. Richard Munro
Chairman of the Board: Ralph P. Davidson
Corporate Editor: Jason McManus
Group Vice President, Books: Reginald K. Brack Jr.
Vice President, Books: George Artandi

TIME-LIFE BOOKS INC.

EDITOR: George Constable
Executive Editor: George Daniels
Director of Design: Louis Klein
Editorial Board: Roberta Conlan, Ellen Phillips,
Gerry Schremp, Gerald Simons, Rosalind Stubenberg,
Kit van Tulleken, Henry Woodhead
Editorial General Manager: Neal Goff
Director of Research: Phyllis K. Wise
Director of Photography: John Conrad Weiser

PRESIDENT: Reginald K. Brack Jr.
Senior Vice President: William Henry
Vice Presidents: Stephen L. Bair, Robert A. Ellis,
John M. Fahey Jr., Juanita T. James,
Christopher T. Linen, James L. Mercer,
Joanne A. Pello, Paul R. Stewart

The Civil War

Series Director: Henry Woodhead
Designer: Herbert H. Quarmby
Series Administrator: Philip Brandt George

Editorial Staff for *Rebels Resurgent*
Associate Editors: Thomas A. Lewis (text);
Jeremy Ross (pictures)
Staff Writers: Jan Leslie Cook, Thomas H. Flaherty Jr.,
David S. Thomson
Researchers: Harris J. Andrews, Susan V. Kelly
(principals); Brian C. Pohanka, Andrea E. Reynolds
Assistant Designer: Cynthia T. Richardson
Copy Coordinators: Stephen G. Hyslop,
Anthony K. Pordes
Picture Coordinator: Betty H. Weatherley
Editorial Assistant: Audrey Prior Keir
Special Contributor: Theodore V. Kruckel

Editorial Operations
Design: Ellen Robling (assistant director)
Copy Room: Diane Ullius
Production: Anne B. Landry (director), Celia Beattie
Quality Control: James J. Cox (director), Sally Collins
Library: Louise D. Forstall

Correspondents: Elisabeth Kraemer-Singh (Bonn);
Margot Hapgood, Dorothy Bacon (London);
Miriam Hsia (New York); Maria Vincenza Aloisi,
Josephine du Brusle (Paris); Ann Natanson (Rome).

The Author:
William K. Goolrick was born and raised in Fredericksburg, Virginia. A graduate of the Virginia Military Institute, he served on General George S. Patton Jr.'s staff
during World War II. Goolrick earned his M.A. in English literature at Columbia University, worked for a dec-
ade with *Life* and later became a senior editor of *The Satur-
day Evening Post.* He is a former editor of the Time-Life
Books World War II series.

The Consultants:
Colonel John R. Elting, USA (Ret.), a former Associate
Professor at West Point, is the author of *Battles for Scandi-
navia* in the Time-Life Books World War II series and of
*The Battle of Bunker's Hill, The Battles of Saratoga, Mili-
tary History and Atlas of the Napoleonic Wars* and *American
Army Life.* Co-author of *A Dictionary of Soldier Talk,* he is
also editor of the three volumes of *Military Uniforms in
America, 1755-1867,* and associate editor of *The West Point
Atlas of American Wars.*

William A. Frassanito, a Civil War historian and lecturer
specializing in photograph analysis, is the author of two
award-winning studies, *Gettysburg: A Journey in Time* and
*Antietam: The Photographic Legacy of America's Bloodiest
Day,* and a companion volume, *Grant and Lee, The Virginia Campaigns.* He has also served as chief consultant to the
photographic history series *The Image of War.*

Les Jensen, Curator of the U.S. Army Transportation
Museum at Fort Eustis, Virginia, specializes in Civil War
artifacts and is a conservator of historic flags. He is a
contributor to *The Image of War* series, consultant for
numerous Civil War publications and museums, and a
member of the Company of Military Historians. He was
formerly Curator of the Museum of the Confederacy in
Richmond, Virginia.

Michael McAfee specializes in military uniforms and has
been Curator of Uniforms and History at the West Point
Museum since 1970. A fellow of the Company of Military
Historians, he coedited with Colonel Elting *Long Endure:
The Civil War Years,* and he collaborated with Frederick
Todd on *American Military Equipage.* He is the author of
Artillery of the American Revolution, 1775-1783, and has
written numerous articles for *Military Images Magazine.*

Library of Congress Cataloguing in Publication Data
Goolrick, William K.
  Rebels resurgent.
  (The Civil War)
  Bibliography: p.
  Includes index.
    1. Fredericksburg, Battle of, 1862.
2. Chancellorsville, Battle of, 1863.
I. Time-Life Books.   II. Title.   III. Series.
E474.85.G66 1985   973.7'33   84-23984
ISBN 0-8094-4748-7
ISBN 0-8094-4748-5 (lib. bdg.)

CONTENTS

Herman Haupt (*far right*), the aggressive field commander of the U.S. Military Railroads, controlled three sections of rail (*shown in blue*) in Virginia that were vital to the campaigns of 1862 and early 1863. The Orange & Alexandria carried Federal troops and supplies southwest as far as Culpeper. From Manassas Junction, the Manassas Gap line ran west to Front Royal and Strasburg. Farther south, a segment of the Richmond, Fredericksburg & Potomac linked Aquia Creek, on the Potomac, with Falmouth, across the Rappahannock from Fredericksburg.

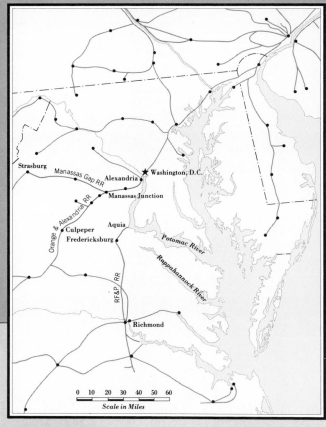

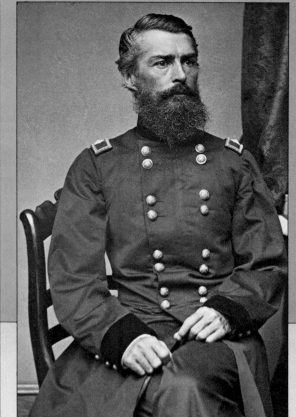

This sprawling yard at Alexandria, Virginia, was the hub of the U.S. Military Railroads. It was linked to nearby Washington by a single bridge over the Potomac.

Gearing the Union's Railroads for War

From the start of the Civil War, the Union had a marked advantage in its railway network. There had been a boom in railway construction during the 1850s, most of it in the Northern states. By 1861, the North had 22,000 miles of track, compared with the South's 9,000 miles; the North had a similar edge in rolling stock—and in the capacity to build more of both.

This asset was not immediately exploited. Railroads never had been used on an ambitious scale to transport and supply armies in the field, and some authorities doubted it could be done — with good reason. Rail systems lacked both uniformity and reliability. Often tracks were built of poor-grade iron rails laid on ties of unseasoned wood; moreover, track gauges varied capriciously from a standard width of 4 feet 8½ inches to widths of 5 and even 6 feet.

Early in 1862 the Union government moved to solve these problems by creating the United States Military Railroads, an agency empowered to coordinate rail service in the North and to control all railroads in occupied territory. To rebuild and run the railroads in war-scarred northern Virginia, Secretary of War Edwin Stanton recruited 45-year-old Herman Haupt.

Haupt was a solemn, outspoken man of prodigious energy. After graduating from West Point at the age of 18, he had resigned his commission to become a civil engineer. Among his many accomplishments, he had helped to survey and build a railroad line across Pennsylvania, and he had written a pioneering book on bridge construction.

Haupt rose eagerly to the new challenge. He demanded freedom from interference by even the most senior officers, although at first he held only a colonel's commission. In short order he built an efficient transportation network, radiating out of Alexandria, Virginia (*below*), to sustain future offensives, including the Fredericksburg and Chancellorsville Campaigns. His success assured a parade of beleaguered Union generals that, whatever else might go wrong, at least the railroads would run on time.

A Bustling Hub for Supply Missions

As field boss of the U.S. Military Railroads, Haupt was responsible for supplying and transporting the Federal armies in Virginia while maintaining the rail lines and rolling stock that made those missions possible. Setting up headquarters at the Alexandria rail yard, he purchased additional locomotives, freight cars and rails, and established a Construction Corps to lay track, build bridges and run the repair shops.

The corps was staffed at first by 300 soldiers, but Haupt preferred civilian workers, and he hired them in increasing numbers. He organized the corps into 10-man squads by skills: teamsters, woodcutters, carpenters and mechanics. Haupt had no time for slackers. Anyone unwilling to work 16 continuous hours when necessary was sent packing.

A steam-powered sawmill at Alexandria cuts up timber for use as ties and as fuel for locomotives.

Carpenters of Haupt's Construction Corps plane the edges of wooden planks by hand at the Alexandria lumberyard.

Damaged rails and iron wheels salvaged from wooden cars are collected at Alexandria, where they will be repaired or melted down for recasting.

The spanking-new wood-burning locomotive *J. H. Devereux*, named for Colonel Haupt's deputy, stands outside the Alexandria roundhouse attended by its crew.

Prefabricated bridge trusses, a Haupt invention, were called "shad bellies" for their fishlike shape. Each 60-foot span could support a load of 108,000 pounds.

Flatcars are loaded with new rails from the abundant stockpile in Alexandria to replace those torn up by Confederate raiders or by retreating Federal troops.

Men of the Construction Corps excavate a siding in occupied Virginia. A locomotive named for the newly promoted General Haupt stands by to haul away earth.

Building with Speed and Ingenuity

Haupt's pressing assignment in May of 1862 was to rebuild the railroad from the mouth of Aquia Creek, on the Potomac, 13 miles to Falmouth, across from Fredericksburg. Retreating Confederates had wrecked the line, reducing the railhead at Aquia Creek to ruins, tearing up miles of track and burning three bridges. The road-bed itself had been churned by cavalry and turned into a quagmire by constant rain.

Haupt put his newly formed Construction Corps to work around the clock. "I threw out a dragnet and raked in all the lanterns to be found," he wrote. "We unloaded iron by candlelight, put it on cars hauled by soldiers to the end of the track, and kept on laying and spiking all night."

The most daunting obstacle in the path of the Construction Corps was a chasm 80 feet deep at Potomac Creek. Haupt

spanned it with a bridge constructed mostly of fresh-cut logs.

It was perilous work. "We got three men at different times in the river, but fished them out," Haupt reported to the War Department. "A fourth is missing, supposed to be drowned."

After only 21 days of labor, the railroad had been restored and Federal supply trains were chugging along it every hour.

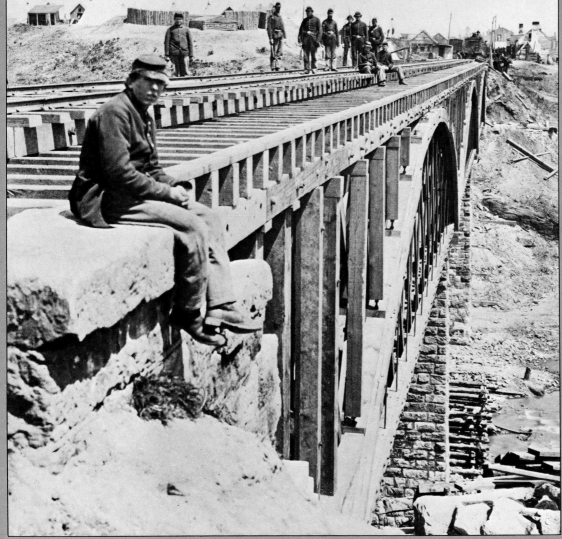

Haupt designed and built the 400-foot-long trestle bridge across Potomac Creek (*above*) in nine days, using two million feet of green lumber and a crew of inexperienced soldiers. President Lincoln, on a visit, called it "the most remarkable structure that human eyes ever rested on. There is nothing in it but beanpoles and cornstalks." In 1863 Haupt replaced it with a sturdier truss bridge (*left*); the replacement was accomplished, he wrote, "without delaying a single train for a single minute."

A Federal work party inspects the damage to the bridge across Bull Run, a vulnerable link on the Orange & Alexandria line near Manassas.

Restoration proceeds quickly on the Bull Run bridge; during the War the span was destroyed six times by military action and once by flood.

A rainy-day detail of soldiers and civilians checks out the rebuilt bridge. Shad-belly trusses now support the span, although the original trestles remain in place.

A crude hoist on the wharf in Alexandria *(top)* raised or lowered a section of track, as the water level dictated, so that rolling stock could be loaded onto barges *(bottom)* for towing down the Potomac.

The Waterborne Railway

In midautumn of 1862, Haupt received orders to transport unprecedented quantities of food, forage and munitions from depots near Washington to the Federal forces assembling near Fredericksburg.

No rail line connected the two places, but Haupt had set up a supply route down the Potomac River to Aquia Creek and from there by rail to the Fredericksburg area. He also devised a way to avoid the tedious unloading of freight at the transfer points between land and water. His trains ran to the river's edge at Alexandria. There the cars were pushed onto flat-bottomed barges.

Two barges bolted together could hold eight freight cars. Four of them could ferry a typical 16-car train 35 miles to the landing at Aquia Creek in six hours, and put it ashore, ready to roll.

On the rebuilt landing at Aquia Creek, a Federal supply train *(left foreground)* that has arrived by river is poised to steam toward Fredericksburg.

Railway agents at a forward supply depot gather before crates of food, which had the highest priority on the Federal rail lines. These civilian employees took orders only from Haupt, who in turn told them: "The railroad is entirely under your control. No military officer has any right to interfere with it."

At Stoneman's Station, outside Falmouth, Virginia, commissary wagons line up at the quartermaster's freight-car office (left) to load provisions recently arrived by rail.

Frustrations down the Line

In November of 1862, Herman Haupt informed Major General Ambrose Burnside in no uncertain terms what Burnside's Army of the Potomac must do if the military supply trains were to sustain the imminent Fredericksburg offensive. First, Haupt said, the army would have to protect the trains from Confederate raiders. Second, the trains would have to run according to a fixed timetable. This meant that the incoming supplies would have to be unloaded promptly and the empty freight cars sent back at once. "Without this," Haupt warned, "the supply of your army is impossible. No man living can do it."

Although he resented taking instructions from a subordinate, Burnside promised cooperation. Still, frustrations abounded for Haupt. Local Union commanders persisted in using loaded freight cars as warehouses, thereby tying up the rolling stock. One paymaster arrogantly commandeered an empty car to serve as his office and had to be evicted forcibly. Soldiers burned replacement ties to keep warm, and used water intended for locomotive boilers to bathe and to wash their clothes. As a result, wrote Haupt, "many engines were stopped on the road by foamy boilers caused by soapy water."

On one occasion, Haupt went in search of an overdue convoy and discovered that a passenger, the wife of a prominent officer, had halted the lead train while she rested for the night at a nearby farmhouse. Even livestock presented hazards, despite the engines' elaborate cowcatchers. One trainman reported laconically: "Ran over cow — engine, tender and eight cars off track."

But Haupt's system prevailed, and by December of 1862 he was moving 800 tons of supplies a day to Burnside's army, poised before Fredericksburg.

This depot was the terminus of the line from Aquia Creek that supplied the Federal campaigns at Fredericksburg and Chancellorsville in 1862 and 1863.

A work crew on the Manassas Gap line in August 1862 begins the arduous task of salvaging a locomotive derailed by roving Confederates.

A Race to Fredericksburg

1

No military officer in the Civil War resisted promotion more assiduously than did Major General Ambrose E. Burnside during 1862. On three separate occasions that year, President Abraham Lincoln asked Burnside to assume command of the Army of the Potomac, and each time the general demurred on the grounds that he was not competent to handle so large a force. He was content to remain a subordinate under Major General George B. McClellan. But on November 7, when the third offer was tendered, Burnside at first refused — then reversed his decision. It was not ambition, nor any surge of self-confidence, that caused him to change his mind; it was the intelligence that if he continued to balk, the command would go to an officer he detested — Major General Joseph Hooker.

Reluctantly, Burnside took command that same night, replacing his longtime friend McClellan. The dread with which he anticipated his new responsibilities deepened to depression after he read his first order from the general in chief of the Union Army, Henry W. Halleck: "Report the position of your troops, and what you propose doing with them."

It was a straightforward, even elementary request. Yet, as Burnside later commented, "I probably knew less than any other corps commander of the position and relative strengths of the several corps of the army." Moreover, there was no time for him to learn. President Lincoln wanted action, and he wanted it immediately; delay had caused McClellan's downfall.

After 15 months of Confederate success, the fortunes of the Confederacy at last appeared to be on the ebb. In September, General Robert E. Lee's thrust into Maryland had been checked and turned back at Antietam Creek; in October, Confederate advances in the West had been stopped at Corinth, Mississippi, and at Perryville, Kentucky.

There had been a golden opportunity in the aftermath of Antietam for the Federals to shorten the War dramatically by smashing Lee's weakened army, but Lincoln had been unable to spur McClellan to action. Lee had escaped into the Shenandoah Valley and had been left in peace for two months, a respite he had used to reorganize and resupply his battered forces. For some time, Lee had been operating with his nine infantry divisions grouped unofficially into two corps under his most reliable commanders — James Longstreet and Thomas J. "Stonewall" Jackson. In October the Confederate Congress approved Lee's corps organization and created the rank of lieutenant general, to which Longstreet and Jackson were immediately promoted.

At length, the increasingly impatient Lincoln had imposed a plan on McClellan: Chase Lee southward, moving along the eastern slopes of the Blue Ridge Mountains and remaining astride his lines of supply; press him, fight him if an opportunity pre-

General Ambrose E. Burnside strikes a heroic pose before what came to be known as the Burnside Bridge after its capture by his troops at the Battle of Antietam.

sented itself, but at least, said the President, "try to beat him to Richmond on the inside track."

However, McClellan had moved his men with such deliberation that by the time they had inched their way south to Warrenton, Lee had positioned half his army — the corps commanded by Longstreet — in Culpeper 20 miles to the southwest, directly in McClellan's path. Lee's other corps, under Jackson, had remained in the Shenandoah Valley,

posing a threat to the Federals' western flank. At this juncture, a thoroughly disgusted Lincoln had relieved McClellan.

Now the reluctant General Burnside would have to make a painful choice. He could continue the march the President had so firmly suggested, despite the obstacle presented by Longstreet's corps; he could try to get between the two halves of Lee's army and deal with them separately; or he could come up with an alternative plan of action. But the

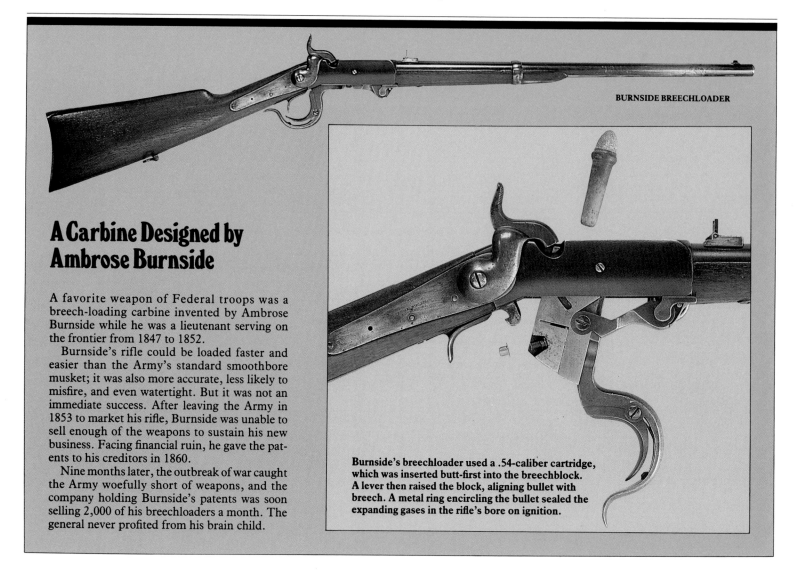

BURNSIDE BREECHLOADER

A Carbine Designed by Ambrose Burnside

A favorite weapon of Federal troops was a breech-loading carbine invented by Ambrose Burnside while he was a lieutenant serving on the frontier from 1847 to 1852.

Burnside's rifle could be loaded faster and easier than the Army's standard smoothbore musket; it was also more accurate, less likely to misfire, and even watertight. But it was not an immediate success. After leaving the Army in 1853 to market his rifle, Burnside was unable to sell enough of the weapons to sustain his new business. Facing financial ruin, he gave the patents to his creditors in 1860.

Nine months later, the outbreak of war caught the Army woefully short of weapons, and the company holding Burnside's patents was soon selling 2,000 of his breechloaders a month. The general never profited from his brain child.

Burnside's breechloader used a .54-caliber cartridge, which was inserted butt-first into the breechblock. A lever then raised the block, aligning bullet with breech. A metal ring encircling the bullet sealed the expanding gases in the rifle's bore on ignition.

President was clearly in no mood to be told that the Army of the Potomac was going into winter quarters.

Nothing in Ambrose Burnside's life had prepared him for the enormity of the task he was about to undertake. It was not false modesty that had impelled him to argue his unfitness for the post. Frequently during his career he had been loath to act, and had been plagued by evil luck when he did act.

He had even appeared unwilling to begin life itself; when he was born in 1824 in Liberty, Indiana, he failed to breathe until the attending physician resorted to tickling his nose with a feather. At the age of 18, the year after his mother died, Burnside left school and apprenticed himself to a tailor in order to help support the large family. A year later his father was elected state senator, and managed to get young Ambrose an appointment to West Point. He graduated squarely in the middle of his class in 1847, a year behind his friend McClellan. Burnside received orders to join the U.S. forces fighting in Mexico, but he arrived too late to see action in a war that brought many of his colleagues glory and promotion. For the next six years, Burnside languished in various frontier assignments.

The long years on the frontier gave Burnside a lot of time to muse and tinker, and during this period the young officer invented a breech-loading rifle. In 1853, Burnside resigned from the army to manufacture his new weapon. He settled in Bristol, Rhode Island, with his bride, a young lady from Providence. (His first attempt at marriage had ended unfortunately. While on leave two years before, he had conducted a whirlwind romance back home in Indiana, become engaged, and even escorted his intended down the aisle. But when asked at the altar if she took this man to be her wedded husband, the bride-to-be had brought the proceedings to a halt by answering with a firm "No!")

By 1855, Burnside's Bristol Firearms Company was a financial disaster, and he was nearly bankrupt. Desperate, he sought help from McClellan, who had also left the Army and was now vice president of the Illinois Central Railroad. McClellan not only got Burnside a job with the railroad, but for a time took the unfortunate inventor and his wife into his home.

Then came the War. Immediately after the fall of Fort Sumter, Burnside took command of the 1st Rhode Island Infantry and marched it to Washington. He led a brigade at Bull Run that July, performed adequately, and was subsequently awarded a brigadier's star. He made his reputation early in 1862 when he commanded a force that conquered Roanoke Island and New Bern, on the coast of North Carolina. His achievement provided one of the few bright spots in the Federal effort thus far, and secured for the Union a vital base of operations on the Southern coast. It also secured for Burnside a promotion to major general, the command of the Army's IX Corps and the confidence of the President. Yet at Antietam, where Burnside commanded the Federal left wing, he showed little dash and probably lost an opportunity to strike Lee a decisive blow.

Whatever his fellow officers and subordinates thought of Burnside's abilities, and the opinions were remarkably diverse, almost everyone agreed that he had a captivating personality. There was a certain brigandish air about his casual dress, the pistol slung

BRIG. GEN. MARSENA PATRICK   BRIG. GEN. EDWARD FERRERO   MAJ. GEN. JOHN PARKE   UNIDENTIFIED STAFF OFFICER

BRIG. GEN. HENRY J. HUNT   BRIG. GEN. WINFIELD SCOTT HANCOCK   MAJ. GEN. DARIUS COUCH   MAJ. GEN. AMBROSE BURNSIDE

Ambrose Burnside and his senior generals commemorate his appointment as army commander with this photograph taken in camp at Warrenton. Several of the men pictured here bitterly opposed the removal of General McClellan, but nevertheless rallied around the affable Burnside. As Brigadier General Winfield Scott Hancock wrote, "We are serving no one man; we are serving our country."

BRIG. GEN. JOHN COCHRANE   BRIG. GEN. SAMUEL STURGIS

BRIG. GEN. ORLANDO WILLCOX   BRIG. GEN. JOHN BUFORD

low on his hip, the broad-brimmed hat atop his balding, impressive head. He smiled frequently, remembered names, looked after the welfare of his troops, won friends with ease, took orders well and conveyed to the world an air of sturdy competence. His extravagant cheek whiskers became known throughout the army by a play upon his name — sideburns.

But Burnside's dashing appearance disguised some critical flaws in his character. He was obstinate, unimaginative, and unsuited both intellectually and emotionally for high command. Those who knew him sensed it eventualiy. "You would think he had a great deal more intelligence than he really possessed," remarked Assistant Secretary of War Charles A. Dana. "You had to know him some time before you really took his measure." Colonel Francis W. Palfrey of the 20th Massachusetts ventured the opinion that "few men, probably, have risen so high upon so slight a foundation as he."

It is to Burnside's credit that he understood his limitations and freely confessed them. And it is an enduring tragedy that his superiors did not listen to him.

But Lincoln needed a leader for the Army of the Potomac, and he had few men from which to choose. The other eligible corps commanders all had disqualifying flaws: Edwin V. Sumner, at 65, was too old; William B. Franklin was uninspired and too much imbued with what Lincoln had called McClellan's "slows"; Hooker was troublesome and too junior in rank. Burnside, on the other hand, was a brave, loyal and youthful officer, one who had done well in North Carolina and seemed free of McClellan's influence despite their friendship. As so often happened in this War, Lincoln was forced to choose not the ideal man for the command, but the one who presented the fewest apparent liabilities.

Burnside's new responsibilities made him physically ill, but he attacked his problems vigorously nevertheless, and on November 9 forwarded to Washington a bold new strategy for the capture of Richmond. He proposed concentrating his forces along the route southwest toward Gordonsville to convince Lee that the Federals intended to continue their drive in that direction. Then Burnside would move his army rapidly southeastward from Warrenton to Fredericksburg, on the Rappahannock River. Burnside explained that by shifting toward the east the army would stay closer to Washington and its base of supplies. It would also be on a more direct route to Richmond, for Fredericksburg stood on the main road midway between the two capitals. Burnside aimed to cross the Rappahannock, take Fredericksburg before Lee could block him, then move south and seize Richmond.

Burnside knew that everything depended on speed; the attack on Fredericksburg, he stipulated, should be made "as soon as the army arrives in front of the place." To streamline his operations, he proposed to reorganize his command by creating three "grand divisions," as he labeled them, each containing two corps and each with its own staff. To command the grand divisions he would name three major generals: Sumner, Franklin and Hooker. At their disposal were well over 100,000 troops.

The rest of Burnside's proposal dealt with the problems of supplying his enormous army. He requested that 30 canalboats and barges be loaded with goods and sent down the Potomac to a new supply base at Belle Plain, 10 miles northeast of Fredericksburg. He wanted additional wagon trains of supplies along with a huge herd of beef cattle to move overland from Alexandria to the Rappahannock crossing. And most important, Burnside asked for enough pontoons to build several floating bridges across the Rappahannock.

The reorganization of the army was immediately approved, but there was little enthusiasm in Washington for Burnside's plan of action. Halleck came to Warrenton to talk with Burnside on November 12 and apparently argued for the Gordonsville line of advance to Richmond. But he did not express his opinion officially, and left the decision to the President. Lincoln was skeptical. He had tried for months to get McClellan to close in and fight the Confederate army, and now the new commander was proposing to skirt that army and move on the Confederate capital. But in the end Lincoln gave his approval, commenting succinctly that the plan "will succeed, if you move very rapidly; otherwise not."

The start of the campaign was propitious. Sumner's grand division led the way, setting off from the Warrenton area at dawn on November 15 — a day ahead of the other two grand divisions — and moving fast. Just after dark two days later, his advance elements marched into the town of Falmouth, situated on the north bank of the Rappahannock little more than a mile upriver from Fredericksburg. Franklin soon reached Stafford Court House, eight miles from Falmouth, and Hooker halted at Hartwood, just seven miles away.

It was a stunning change from the McClellan days. As a correspondent for the New

York *Tribune* wrote on November 18, "Officers wont to believe that a great command cannot move more than six miles a day, and accustomed to our old method of waiting a week for the issue of new clothing or a month for the execution of an order to advance, rub their eyes in mute astonishment. We have marched from Warrenton forty miles, in two days and a half."

Burnside seemed to be justifying the trust placed in him: In command for less than two weeks, he had formulated a plan, reorganized his army and commenced a campaign, and now his troops stood poised at their first objective. Better yet, Fredericksburg and the heights beyond it were held by just four companies of Confederate infantry, a cavalry regiment and a battery of light artillery. Longstreet's corps was still 30 miles away at Culpeper, and Jackson's corps remained in the Shenandoah. All Burnside had to do was get his forces across the Rappahannock quickly and the town was his. The ingredients for a major Federal triumph were all there. Yet Burnside hesitated.

Two of his generals urged him to strike immediately. Sumner, who had learned of a ford not far upstream from Falmouth, asked permission to cross at once and occupy Fredericksburg. But the weather was threatening, and the rivers were already high; Burnside worried that any force cross-

Zouaves of the 5th New York gather for Sunday prayer in camp near Warrenton on November 16, 1862, not long before they joined the Federal advance on Fredericksburg. A crack outfit, the Zouaves had been weakened by months of hard campaigning.

ing the river might be trapped on the opposite bank by high water, and rejected Sumner's request. Arriving at Falmouth on the 19th, Burnside inspected the ford and concluded that his decision had been correct; the river was already too high for infantry or artillery to cross safely, although cavalry could get over.

General Hooker also proposed to cross, even farther upriver at a place called United States Ford. Then, according to a scheme of his own devising, he would strike out for Bowling Green, south of Fredericksburg and only 35 miles from Richmond. Not content to make the suggestion to Burnside alone,

Hooker — in an act of stunning insubordination — sent a letter directly to Secretary of War Edwin M. Stanton explaining his idea and criticizing Burnside for his hesitancy. Hooker proposed that the Secretary take a hand in arranging for supplies, and presumed to sign the letter — to a high official he had met only once — as "Your friend." Stanton never replied, Burnside rejected the proposal as premature, and Hooker's gaffe was ignored — for the time being.

Robert E. Lee knew that something was afoot, but he could not decide just what it was. He had a reputation for being able

An unseasonable blizzard in November 1862 lashes at troops of the 2nd U.S. Cavalry near Waterloo, Virginia. The cavalrymen, led by Brigadier General Alfred Pleasonton, were scouting for the Army of the Potomac as it pursued Robert E. Lee's forces south after the battle at Antietam.

to divine an opposing commander's intentions, but then McClellan had been extremely predictable. In fact, Lee had lamented McClellan's departure. "We always understood each other so well," he remarked to Longstreet. "I fear they may continue to make these changes till they find someone whom I don't understand."

It was beginning to look as if Burnside was such an opponent. Lee learned of Sumner's departure from Warrenton on November 15, but was uncertain what it portended. His confusion, augmented by fragmentary and false intelligence reports, lasted for several days. At one point Lee seemed to believe that Burnside intended to take his army to Alexandria, put it aboard ships, and sail it to North Carolina.

Then at nightfall on November 17, Lee learned that Sumner's brigades were approaching Fredericksburg. "I do not know whether this movement on Fredericksburg is intended as a feint or a real advance upon Richmond," he admitted to Confederate Secretary of War George W. Randolph. In the latter case, Lee promised, "this whole army will be in position."

Lee ordered Longstreet to send out two divisions from Culpeper on the 18th. One, under Brigadier General Robert Ransom, moved south along the Orange & Alexandria Railroad toward the North Anna River, south of Fredericksburg, to get into position to block the Federals there if need be. The other, under Major General Lafayette McLaws, marched eastward toward Fredericksburg. Brigadier General William Henry Fitzhugh Lee's cavalry brigade and Brigadier General James H. Lane's artillery were also sent to Fredericksburg. The Confederate commander suggested to Jackson —

Lee seldom gave his gifted subordinate a direct order — that he might move a few of his divisions east of the Blue Ridge to be closer at hand. And the cavalry under Major General James Ewell Brown (Jeb) Stuart was sent north across the Rappahannock to scout the enemy movements. On that same day one of Stuart's troopers reported that Burnside's entire army was moving toward Fredericksburg. Lee immediately intercepted Ransom's division and diverted it north to the Rappahannock.

But Lee was still unsure of Burnside's intentions, and remained unwilling to have Jackson abandon the Shenandoah Valley entirely. Jackson had reported that the Federals might be advancing from Harpers Ferry, and Lee worried that with Jackson gone, the Shenandoah could be laid waste.

Lee was certain of only one thing: He did not want to fight at Fredericksburg. He preferred to make a stand against Burnside 25 miles farther south along the North Anna River. There his men would have a more favorable position to defend and there, too, the Federal lines of communication would be greatly extended. But as always, Lee would remain flexible. Much would depend on what Longstreet found.

Longstreet had ridden out at the head of McLaws' division on that wintry day of November 18. On the next day Lee ordered the divisions of Major Generals George Pickett, John B. Hood and Richard H. Anderson to move toward Fredericksburg. The road from Culpeper led across the Rappahannock at a ford where the icy water was three feet deep. Many of the men removed shoes and pants before they braved the numbing cold of the water, only to learn that they must cross the deeper, even colder Rapidan one

Pontoons ordered by General
Burnside to bridge the Rappahannock
are hauled from Aquia Creek to
the army encampment at Falmouth.

mile ahead. So they simply marched on, carrying their clothes, bare limbs glistening in the weak winter sun.

At the Rapidan, Brigadier General Joseph B. Kershaw of South Carolina rode across and waited for his men on the other side. "Go ahead, boys, don't mind this," he shouted, warm and dry atop his steed. Then he began to reminisce about the days of the war in Mexico, when campaigning was really tough. His troops would have none of that, however. "General," one of the men shouted, "it wasn't so cold in Mexico." Another chimed in: "Nor did they fight a war in winter." That was enough to silence Kershaw, and the troops shivered their way along the road to Fredericksburg.

As the Confederates were taking up their positions in the heights behind Fredericksburg on November 20, Longstreet recalled, they found the town's inhabitants "in a state of great excitement" — the Federals were across the river. The agitation of the populace increased the next day, November 21, when the Union's General Sumner dispatched a curt note to Fredericksburg's mayor and council. "Under cover of the houses of your city," it read, "shots have been fired upon the troops of my command. Your mills and manufactories are furnishing provisions and the material for clothing for armed bodies in rebellion against the Government of the United States. Your railroads and other means of transportation are removing supplies to depots of such troops." If the authorities did not surrender the city, Sumner continued, he would give them 16 hours to evacuate noncombatants and then he would begin a bombardment.

Longstreet, for his part, assured the townspeople that he did not intend to occupy Fredericksburg for military purposes, but warned them that he would not permit the Federals to enter it without a fight. In the end, the mayor promised to stop the sniping and the furnishing of military supplies to the Confederate troops, and Sumner withdrew his ultimatum.

Lee was dismayed to find that with his few divisions he was facing the entire Army of the Potomac across the river. He was also puzzled by the Federals' inactivity. For 48 hours, Burnside's grand divisions had confronted only token opposition in Fredericksburg. Why had they not attacked?

Since his arrival at Falmouth, Burnside had encountered so many problems that he seemed to take little notice of his enemy. His fears about the weather were confirmed when heavy rain began to fall on the afternoon of the 19th, and continued through the 20th and the 21st. Burnside tried to keep his grand divisions poised to move "rapidly and on an hour's notice," as an order of the 20th read, but in the face of the rising river and deepening mud, rapid movement was hardly possible. Furthermore, he was concerned that his overland supply routes from Belle Plain and nearby Aquia Creek on the Potomac were not yet fully in operation. But most of all, the general was distressed to find that the pontoons he had called for so urgently had not yet arrived.

Burnside thought he had made it very clear to Halleck in their meeting at Warrenton on November 12 that he intended to march down the north side of the Rappahannock and cross the river at Falmouth. Halleck, on the other hand, was under the impression that Burnside had agreed to modify his plan, so that the army would cross the river at a ford upstream from Fredericksburg, then march along the south bank. In that case, there obviously would be little urgency about the pontoons, and Halleck did not immediately act on Burnside's request for them.

Not until November 14 did word of Burnside's need for the pontoons reach Brigadier General Daniel P. Woodbury, who was responsible for virtually all of the pontoon-bridge materials in the army. Woodbury ordered Major Ira Spaulding of the 50th New York Engineers to prepare two shipments of pontoons, to be sent on different routes in hopes that at least one would make it. One load of 48 pontoons was to be shipped down the Potomac River to Belle Plain, then hauled overland to Burnside. On the way, however, the steamer towing the pontoons was delayed; it did not reach Belle Plain until November 18. Then it turned out that no one had arranged for the teams and special wagons needed to haul the pontoons to Falmouth. It would take another six days to get them to Burnside, just eight miles away.

The other pontoon shipment, sent by wagon train from Washington, was likewise bungled. The harnesses that Spaulding ordered for the teams arrived unassembled in boxes and had to be put together before they could be used. Then some of the 270 horses furnished by the quartermaster turned out to be unbroken to harness. As a result, Spaulding could not get the wagon train under way until the afternoon of November 19. And by then, the heavy rain had turned even the best roads into mires of clinging Virginia mud. The teams would manage five miles a day at best.

Deciding on November 22 that he would never make it overland, Spaulding determined instead to tow the pontoons down the Potomac to Belle Plain. He asked for a steamer to meet him at the mouth of Occoquan Creek, 15 miles south of Alexandria. Spaulding first had to build a bridge with the pontoons to get his horses and wagons across the Occoquan so they could go on to Belle Plain by land. Then he dismantled the bridge and made rafts of the pontoons. When he had floated this makeshift fleet to the mouth of the creek, he had to wait for high tide before he could get his rafts through the shallows and out to the waiting steamer in the Potomac. The pontoons finally reached the Belle Plain wharf just before dark on November 24. Spaulding found teams ready for him, and by 10 a.m. on November 25 the pontoons were loaded and on their way. Five hours later they rolled into Falmouth.

General Woodbury had reached Falmouth with the other shipment of pontoons the day before, and the furious Burnside had ordered the officer arrested and held until he could give a "satisfactory explanation" of the delays. The astonished Woodbury quickly did so, and Burnside calmed down. Woodbury was released, but both he and Halleck were blamed by the press.

Burnside at last had his pontoons and could build his bridges. Moreover, the rail line from Aquia Creek was open, thanks to the herculean labors of the quartermas-

ters and the Army's Construction Corps.

But time had run out. Burnside, watching the steady swelling of the Confederate forces across the river, was having second thoughts about an immediate frontal attack. Now the Federals would have to cross the Rappahannock, he later wrote in his official report, "in the face of a vigilant and formidable foe."

President Jefferson Davis had made it clear to Lee by the time the general reached Fredericksburg on the 20th that he wanted Burnside stopped there rather than at the North Anna River, closer to Richmond. Although Lee did not like the look of things, he obediently began to deploy his army for the defense of the city.

He did not for a moment consider mounting a defense of the town proper; Federal artillery deployed along Stafford Heights, on the far bank of the river, made that impossible. But just behind Fredericksburg a long, wooded ridge offered an excellent natural defensive position. Beginning at the Rappahannock north of the town, the ridge formed a gentle crescent that curved south and east for a distance of about seven miles. Rising at its highest point to 150 feet, it was for the most part beyond the range of the Federal guns, and could be made formidable by the construction of rifle pits and earthworks.

Along this ridge Lee placed Longstreet's divisions, the last of which arrived on November 23 — Anderson on the far left; then McLaws, just behind Fredericksburg itself; then Pickett, across a low-lying area on either side of a creek called Deep Run; then Hood on the far right. Ransom's division was held in reserve, and a single brigade was deployed in the town to harass any attempted crossing. Finally, on November 26, Lee sent for Jackson.

Typically, Jackson had anticipated his commander's wishes and had marched his troops out of Winchester early on November 22. He led the men southwest for New Market, then east across the Blue Ridge at Fisher's Gap.

As the long Confederate column toiled through the mountains, Captain James F. J. Caldwell of the 1st South Carolina marveled at the spectacle. "Ascending and descending the mountains was grand," he recalled, "the long line being visible for miles, as it wound up and down and around, with glittering arms and accoutrements, like some huge serpent with silver scales, dragging its tortuous folds along." In the evening, Caldwell continued, he could see "a thousand bivouac fires flashing and glowing on the mountain side, while weary soldiers rested and warmed and chatted after the labors of the day."

As usual, Stonewall Jackson set a grueling pace — an average of 20 miles a day. Crossing the Blue Ridge, the troops reached Madison Court House on the 25th of November, and were concentrated around Orange Court House on the 27th. On November 29, in the midst of a heavy snowstorm, Jackson arrived at Lee's tent.

Camping in the woods, a refugee family from Fredericksburg bids an emotional farewell to a young man returning to fight with Lee's Confederates. A newspaper reported that about 6,000 residents fled the city for the safety of the countryside, where most had to live on "such scanty and precarious subsistance as is at hand."

Traffic between the Lines

As the armies massed for battle along the Rappahannock, Confederate and Union soldiers engaged in a lively if illicit commerce across the river. The woefully ill-supplied Confederates coveted coffee, sugar, overcoats and shoes — items Federals willingly gave up in exchange for Southern tobacco.

The Rappahannock presented no obstacle to determined and innovative traders. Rigging a wire across the river near a burned-out bridge, men pulled items of exchange back and forth on a trolley. At a ford above Falmouth, men of the 4th Georgia and 8th Alabama waded through icy water holding haversacks stuffed with tobacco, which they swapped for treasured articles with men of the 4th New York.

A miniature trading fleet of rafts and makeshift boats also plied the waters of the Rappahannock, bearing goods from one side to the other. Invariably, Confederates would christen their vessels *Virginia*, after the ironclad known in the North as the *Merrimac*. And just as often, a craft on its return voyage would be relabeled *Monitor*.

In time, the troops established rates of exchange for the most valuable commodities, coffee and tobacco. Enterprising Confederate soldiers would swap 10 pounds of tobacco, which brought $2.50 a pound, for one Federal overcoat. The overcoats were then sent south to Richmond, where each sold for a whopping $100.

On the north bank of the Rappahannock, Union pickets launch a shingle fitted with a paper sail and laden with a cargo of coffee. Confederates across the river wait to return the vessel with tobacco.

A Confederate's scrawled message, shipped aboard a small boat at Fredericksburg, requests coffee and stamps in trade. Officers on both sides generally overlooked such illegal bartering by the troops.

Federals and Confederates negotiate a trade of coffee for tobacco. Such deals reduced animosity between the two sides. A Confederate who swam the Rappahannock with a load of tobacco reported that the Federals greeted him with "no chaffing or bantering, only roistering welcomes."

Lee quickly deployed Jackson's troops, sending Major General Daniel Harvey Hill's division 18 miles downriver to Port Royal, and Brigadier General Jubal Early's division to Skinker's Neck, 12 miles downriver. The division of Major General Ambrose Powell Hill was deployed at Yerby's House, six and a half miles southeast of Fredericksburg, and that of Brigadier General William B. Taliaferro at Guinea Station, four and a half miles south of town. The four commands were to guard against any attempt by Burnside to cross downstream and outflank the Confederates. Meanwhile, Stuart's four brigades of cavalry guarded the army's front and flanks.

Lee's Army of Northern Virginia, 72,564 strong, was at last in place. It faced, across the Rappahannock, 116,683 men of the Army of the Potomac. Never before or afterward in this War would so many armed men confront each other.

And between the two mighty engines of destruction huddled the forlorn little town. "No people were in the place," Longstreet wrote later, "except aged and infirm men, and women and children."

When it became obvious that a battle was inevitable, the Confederates told those civilians remaining in Fredericksburg that they had better leave. "The evacuation of the place by the distressed women and helpless men was a painful sight," Longstreet wrote. "Many were almost destitute and had nowhere to go, but, yielding to the cruel necessities of war, they collected their portable effects and turned their back on the town. Many were forced to seek shelter in the woods and brave the icy November nights to escape the approaching assault from the Federal army."

While Burnside pondered his next move and Lee waited for him to make it, an unofficial truce prevailed among the soldiers on either side of the Rappahannock. Occasionally a picket fired across the 400-foot-wide river, rarely with effect, and usually just to taunt the foe. When shots rang out above Falmouth one night, a Confederate picket yelled across the water, "Say, Yanks, there are some fools shooting across the river up above, but we won't shoot if you don't." And so it was agreed.

The lull continued into early December, during which time Burnside conferred with President Lincoln. The President requested a meeting in an exceedingly gentle telegram sent on November 25: "If I should be in boat off Aquia Creek at dark tomorrow (Wednesday) evening, could you, without inconvenience, meet me and pass an hour or two with me?" And on November 28th Burnside apparently traveled to Washington to speak with Lincoln and Halleck. Oddly, no record exists of the details of either conference. But Burnside at last had formulated a new plan of attack, and presumably, he took the opportunity to clear it with his superiors.

He then called a council of his grand division commanders and announced that instead of crossing at Fredericksburg, he would make his move downstream at Skinker's Neck, which his engineers had recommended as a crossing site. Sumner, ever the faithful subordinate, said he would do what he could, and Franklin expressed his readiness. But the obstreperous Hooker flatly opposed the idea, protesting that to attempt to cross a river in the face of the Confederates was preposterous. Burnside brushed aside Hooker's objections.

But the events of the next few days caused Burnside to rethink his strategy. The commander called up Federal gunboats from Port Royal to support the attack. But on December 4, Confederate shore batteries at Skinker's Neck succeeded in driving the gunboats back downstream. Then Federal spotters, venturing aloft in hydrogen balloons, detected Jubal Early's and D. H. Hill's divisions in their camps near Skinker's Neck and Port Royal.

The discovery of thousands of Confederates waiting at the intended crossing point convinced Burnside that Lee had guessed the Federal strategy. In fact, Lee had made preparations for every contingency, and had realized immediately that a wide sweep against his right would be the most effective move Burnside could make. Burnside, underestimating Lee's flexibility and assuming that the Confederate general had weakened his center in order to strengthen his right, decided to revert to his original battle plan: He would cross his main force at Fredericksburg after all. Explaining the change to Halleck after the battle, Burnside said he believed that the enemy "did not anticipate the crossing of our whole force at Fredericksburg; and I hoped, by rapidly throwing the whole command over at that place, to separate, by a vigorous attack, the forces of the enemy on the river below from the forces behind and on the crests in the rear of the town."

Late on the night of December 9, Burnside notified headquarters in Washington of his change of plans, and pleaded at the same time for reassurance. Burnside's message concluded with a note directed to Halleck personally: "The movement is so important that I feel anxious to be fortified

Major General Lafayette McLaws, one of Lee's most dogged defensive fighters, was ideally suited to command the troops dug in on the heights behind Fredericksburg. One of McLaws' junior officers once likened him to a Roman centurion who "stood at his post in Herculaneum until the lava ran over him."

by his approval. Please answer." No answer was ever sent.

Burnside's agony of uncertainty could hardly have been eased by the results of two additional conferences he convened to explain his plan and to ask for support from his fellow officers. He knew that most of them now opposed his plan, he said, and reiterated that he had not wanted this command, but he had it just the same. "Your duty is not to throw cold water," he said, "but to aid me loyally with your advice and hearty service." At a later meeting he explained what he wanted them to do, and at length Brigadier General William H. French enthusiastically predicted the battle would be won within 48 hours, then led three cheers for the commanding general.

Burnside casually asked two junior officers what they thought of his strategy. According to an account by one of the officers, Colonel Rush C. Hawkins of the 9th New York, the replies were brutally frank. "If you make the attack as contemplated," Colonel Hawkins told him, "it will be the greatest slaughter of the war; there isn't infantry enough in our whole army to carry those heights if they are well defended." Surprised and irritated, Burnside turned to Lieutenant Colonel Joseph H. Taylor for his comments. Taylor was equally forthright: "The carrying out of your plan will be murder, not warfare."

As his officers perceived, Burnside's logic was seriously flawed. Lee might not have anticipated the main attack at Fredericksburg — but it was unnecessary to do so. The position he occupied on the heights behind the town was one of the most formidable he and his army would ever hold. He had distributed his forces intelligently, taking great care to provide for rapid lateral movement to counter any maneuver Burnside might undertake.

Moreover, Lee could not be surprised: Burnside would have to build his pontoon bridges in full view of the Confederates, cross his regiments one after another in long lines, and then battle Lee's skirmishers in the streets before Federal forces could even approach the main Confederate line. At best, the preliminary movements would take several hours — more likely an entire day — and Burnside was fully aware that Lee had several divisions within an easy march of Fredericksburg.

Yet this knowledge left Burnside undeterred. "Oh! I know where Lee's forces are, and I expect to surprise him," he declared. "I expect to cross and occupy the hills before Lee can bring anything serious to meet me."

The attack was set for the morning of December 11. The day before, the men were issued three days' rations and 60 rounds of ammunition each. A massive wagon train with another 12 days' rations for the army stood ready on Stafford Heights, indicative of Burnside's boast that he would walk over Lee's defenses and soon be on the road to Richmond.

That evening, despite the bitter cold, a Federal band set up at the edge of the partially iced-over Rappahannock near the ruins of the railroad bridge, burned earlier in the War. Both armies listened as the band played "Hail Columbia," "The Star Spangled Banner," "Yankee Doodle" and other tunes familiar since childhood to men of both the Union and the Confederacy. Then the musicians paused, perhaps thinking there would be a response in kind from the southern shore. Hearing nothing, the Federals struck up "Dixie," and cheers and laughter from men in blue and gray rippled along both sides of the Rappahannock.

Confederate General McLaws, listening from the ridge above Fredericksburg, did not enjoy the interlude. He suspected that the serenade might be an attempt to lull his division into complacency. That same night the general inspected his pickets along the riverbank, and ordered them to dig more rifle pits. Even before the cheering and laughter died away, his troops were grimly preparing for battle.

Swift Signals via Flag and Telegraph

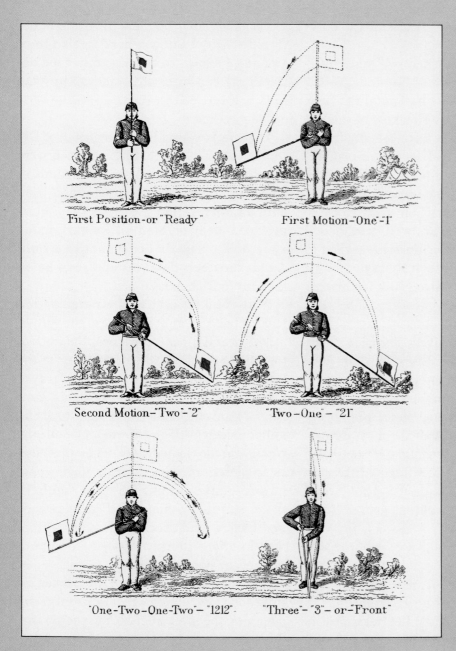

First Position-or "Ready"

First Motion-"One"-"1"

Second Motion-"Two"-"2"

"Two-One" - "21"

"One-Two-One-Two"- "1212"

"Three"-"3"-or-"Front"

A page from Albert Myer's *Manual of Signals* shows part of his flag code. A dip of the flag to the left stood for the numeral 1, a dip to the right meant 2. Combinations of the numbers stood for letters; 21 equaled *O*, for example, and 1212 indicated *P*. A forward dip of the flag meant 3. A single 3 marked the end of a word, 22 the end of a sentence, and 333 the end of a message.

On the eve of the Battle of Fredericksburg, General Ambrose Burnside deployed for the first time in history a military unit — the nascent U.S. Army Signal Corps — equipped with both flags and an electric telegraph for sending messages in the field. Stationed on hills overlooking the battlefield, observers used flags to relay information to Burnside's headquarters to the rear. At the same time, signalmen with Burnside flashed orders from the general over telegraph wires to command posts on his left and right flanks. The swift signaling methods — far faster than the dispatch riders employed in the past — did not alter the course of this battle, but they would profoundly affect later Civil War campaigns and change the way future wars would be fought.

The founder of the Signal Corps was a sharply intelligent if irascible New York physician named Albert J. Myer. Shortly after graduating from Buffalo Medical College in 1851, Myer enlisted in the Army and served on posts in the Far West. He soon found himself more interested in signals than in surgery, and devised a system of simple flag wigwags (*left*) by which operators could relay messages across miles of prairie.

Summoned to Washington at the outbreak of war, Myer set up a Signal Corps training school in nearby Georgetown and began outfitting telegraph units that would accompany, in covered wagons, Federal armies in the field. Before the War's end, Myer's men had strung thousands of miles of wire, helping coordinate the movements of huge forces, both on the march and in the heat of battle.

A Signal Corps officer and his men gather on the roof of Army headquarters in Washington, D.C. From here, messages were exchanged with stations in the field. Two of the men hold staffs topped with torches — oil-filled copper cylinders with cotton wicks — that were wigwagged for night messages.

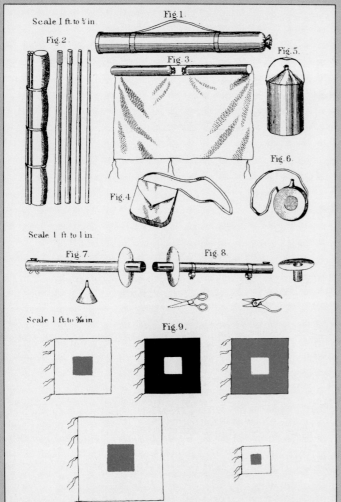

A signalman's kit, as shown in Myer's *Manual*, included several flagstaffs (*Fig. 2*), night torches (*Fig. 7 and Fig. 8*) with a fuel can (*Fig. 5*), and several flags (*Fig. 9*). The flags were always of two colors — white with a red square, or red with a white square — for greater visibility. The largest ones, six feet square, were used for long-distance work.

An illustration from Myer's *Manual* shows how signaling techniques might work together. Stations "C," "D," "E" and "F" on the hilltops would send messages by flag to signal stations "A" and "B." Telegraph operators there would then relay messages by wire to command posts of the encamped army.

Positioned high on a slope, a Federal signal party uses telescopes and binoculars to observe Confederate positions near Fredericksburg in the spring of 1863.

Reconnaissance from Lofty Perches

Stationed on lofty, exposed vantage points, and often in advance of the army, Signal Corpsmen ran a high risk of encountering the Confederates. At the Battle of Antietam, for example, an entire Union flag-signaling outpost was captured during a Confederate counterattack.

The corps's officers were well aware of the danger. Myer's *Manual* instructed that even small scouting parties should throw out advance guards to warn of any hostile approach. Signalmen in danger of capture were ordered above all to shatter their 30-power telescopes. These instruments were invaluable to the Confederates, who could not manufacture high-quality lenses.

Imperfections of a New Technology

Colonel Myer's Signal Corps was nagged at first by problems with the telegraph. The first sets *(right)*, produced for Myer by New York inventor George Beardslee, lacked the power to transmit messages more than five miles. And the uncoated copper wire that carried the current had to be laboriously strung on poles fitted with glass insulators.

More powerful telegraph sets were soon produced, however, along with rubber-coated wire that could be thrown over the branches of trees or bushes, or if necessary, laid on the bare ground. This rugged new wire, Union generals were delighted to discover, could be unreeled almost as fast as their men could march.

Perched precariously atop fresh-cut saplings, members of a telegraph construction crew string wire above the traffic below.

A signalman spells out a
message on a Beardslee telegraph by moving a pointer
to the desired letters. Such
sets, powered by a mag-
neto that the operator
cranked, were in time supplanted by heavier, battery-
powered machines.

Burnside's Uncertain Plan

"During the night, the ground was frozen, and the movements of artillery could be plainly heard through the fog. We were now about to measure our strength with the largest and best-equipped army that had ever stood upon a battle-field in America."

COLONEL E. PORTER ALEXANDER, C.S.A., AT FREDERICKSBURG

The closer drew the time for battle, the more muddled became General Burnside's thinking — as did his communications. His orders to his grand division commanders consisted of little more than rambling verbal instructions. The commanders were told where to cross the Rappahannock: Sumner, on the northern flank, was to cross at Fredericksburg and occupy the town; Hooker's troops were to be held in reserve; and Franklin's men, on the southern flank, were to cross a mile downriver, below the mouth of Deep Run. But what they were to do after that remained unclear as late as December 10, the eve of the movement. Details, Burnside kept saying, would be forthcoming.

The Confederates were far better prepared. Whatever doubts Lee might have had about his ability to understand Burnside were rapidly dissipating. Coolly refusing to be rushed, Lee waited to concentrate his army until Burnside's intentions became crystal clear. In fact, despite the abundant signs of impending action at Fredericksburg, on the night of the 10th four Confederate divisions were still guarding the crossings far downstream.

But Longstreet's corps was firmly in place on the high ground behind Fredericksburg. Anchored on Marye's Heights scarcely a thousand yards from the city, Longstreet's line extended south to Deep Run, then arced along the heights beyond that stream to a place called Captain Hamilton's Crossing, where the Richmond, Fredericksburg & Po-tomac Railroad curved through a gap in the hills. Lee's cavalry, commanded by General Jeb Stuart, was spread out across the bottom land between Hamilton's Crossing and the Rappahannock at its confluence with Massaponax Creek. Along the entire Confederate line, the soldiers had built roads and improved existing ones in order to shift reinforcements rapidly.

The Confederates — though outnumbered and underequipped — were supremely confident. They held the high ground, they had been preparing their defenses for almost three weeks, and they trusted their generals. Moreover, the top commanders themselves — Lee, Longstreet and Jackson — respected one another and communicated well.

In all the Army of the Potomac, by contrast, only the engineers seemed to know exactly what to do. Their task — building five bridges in a few hours for the crossing of 100,000 men plus artillery — was unprecedented in the history of the U.S. Army. Yet Burnside's chief engineer, Lieutenant Cyrus B. Comstock, dealt with all of the complexities in a crisp, eight-paragraph order that remains a model of clarity. He allowed for only one contingency. "If enemy's fire is kept down," he wrote, "bridges to be thrown as soon as boats are unloaded; if too hot, wait till artillery silences it."

Soldiers of the 50th New York Engineers, under Major Ira Spaulding, were to build two bridges at the site of an old rope ferry at the center of Fredericksburg, and another

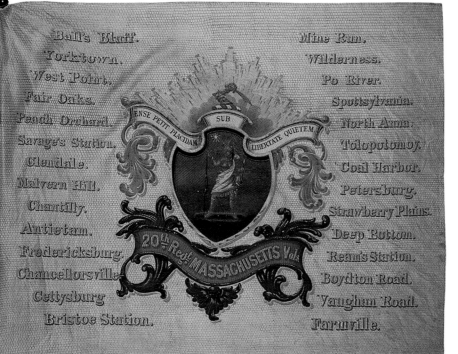

The regimental flag of the 20th Massachusetts lists the battles in which the hard-fighting unit was engaged. At Fredericksburg, after crossing the river in pontoons, the 20th helped storm the town, losing 163 dead and wounded while displaying, in the words of one officer, "unflinching bravery and splendid discipline."

opposite the docks at the lower end of town. Two more bridges at Franklin's crossing point downstream were the responsibility of the men of the 15th New York Engineers, under Major James Magruder, and a battalion of Regular engineers commanded by Lieutenant Charles E. Cross.

The bridge-builders had one of the most dangerous assignments imaginable. Working unarmed, they had to haul their pontoons out into the freezing river, position the flat-bottomed boats in line, moor them securely, lash them together and then lay 400 feet of planking to the opposite shore—all while exposed to enemy fire. They were ordered to begin at 2 a.m. on December 11.

On the Confederate side of the river, Brigadier General William Barksdale rode uneasily up and down the bank, inspecting his pickets and checking for signs of enemy activity. His 1,600 troops—the 13th, 17th and 21st Mississippi Regiments, three companies of the 18th Mississippi and a battalion of the 8th Florida—had been ordered to harass any Federal crossing, slowing it down as long as possible before withdrawing to the main Confederate lines. Barksdale had posted his sharpshooters in rifle pits and basements and behind walls all along the riverfront. From time to time as Barksdale patrolled, he reined in his horse and listened. At length his vigilance was rewarded; he and his anxious men heard the unmistakable creaking and rumbling of heavy equipment being hauled down to the far bank.

Then, long before dawn, Barksdale's men could hear the sounds of pontoons splashing into the river and planks thudding into place. As the bridges were extended in the darkness, Federal engineers could be heard talking in undertones. With the dawn, a mist rising over the river continued to shroud the bridge-builders, some of whom were now within 80 yards of the Confederate sharpshooters. Barksdale told his superiors that he would open fire as soon as he could see his target. Up on Marye's Heights, a cannon barked twice, shattering the early-morning hush and alerting the slumbering Army of Northern Virginia to the long-awaited Federal crossing. The warning signal was at once confirmed by the sound of musketry.

"The enemy opened a galling fire upon us," Major Spaulding of the engineers wrote later, "killing one captain and two men and wounding several others. The infantry supporting us on the flanks were at long range, and could do little damage to the enemy. My men were working without arms, had no means of returning the enemy's fire, and were driven from the work."

The Federal artillery on the heights then

opened fire to drive the Confederates from their riverfront positions. But the sharpshooters were well protected. Burnside's chief of artillery, Brigadier General Henry J. Hunt, ordered 36 guns taken down to the riverside to blaze away at closer range. But when the guns ceased firing after about an hour to let the engineers go back to work, the sharpshooters opened up again and sent the bridge-builders racing back to cover.

This frustrating situation continued until about 1 p.m., when the Federals brought all their available artillery — about 100 guns — to bear on the hapless town. From his vantage point on Marye's Heights, Colonel E. Porter Alexander of the Confederate artillery watched Fredericksburg being reduced to rubble. "The city, except its steeples, was still veiled in the mist which had settled in the valleys," he wrote. "Above it and in it incessantly showed the round white clouds of bursting shells, and out of its midst there soon rose three or four columns of dense black smoke from houses set on fire by the explosions. The atmosphere was so perfectly calm and still that the smoke rose vertically in great pillars for several hundred feet before spreading outward in black sheets."

Watching from a similar vantage point on the opposite side of the river, Chaplain William Locke of the 11th Pennsylvania later recalled his conflicting emotions: "When all the time-honored associations belonging to Fredericksburg were remembered, that a large part of the youth of George Washington was spent there, that for years it was the home of his mother, and her last earthly resting place, we could wish that such a fate had not overtaken this old town." But considering "the bitterness of the present," Locke continued, "there was a subdued satisfaction as the angry flames, approaching from different directions, threatened to leave the doomed city a mass of ruins."

During the next two hours, the Federals fired 5,000 shells into Fredericksburg. The explosions tore gaping holes in brick houses, set wooden houses ablaze, dug craters in streets and gardens, and thoroughly terrified the few citizens remaining. But the bombardment failed to drive off Barksdale's men. When the Federal artillery grew quiet

A train of flat-bottomed pontoons atop carriages sits along a Virginia road. Typically, each of the pontoons was crammed with essential gear: oars, oarlocks, ropes, a boat hook and an anchor.

and the engineers resumed their work, the tenacious Mississippians emerged from their shelters yet again and resumed firing.

Eventually, around 2:30 p.m., General Hunt admitted that his artillery could not dislodge the sharpshooters, and suggested to Burnside that infantrymen be rowed across in pontoons to clear the opposite shore. Burnside agreed. Teams of engineers were assigned to handle the pontoons, and volunteers from the 7th Michigan, the 19th and 20th Massachusetts and the 89th New York clambered into the makeshift assault boats.

As the Federals crossed, they came under heavy fire; one man was killed and several were wounded. But all the pontoons made it to the other side. The men leaped out, formed ranks under the protection of the riverbank, and rushed up the nearest street. Within minutes, they had taken 30 prisoners and cleared the area bordering the bridges. Other Federal units then landed, and the attackers pushed farther into the city.

Nevertheless, the Mississippians had accomplished their mission superbly, holding up General Sumner's entire grand division for the better part of a day. When, around 4:30, Longstreet at last ordered the defenders to withdraw, Barksdale's troops retired street by street, hotly contesting every inch; within a stretch of about 50 yards, the attacking Federals lost 97 officers and men.

One Confederate's zeal proved excessive. A member of the rear guard, Lieutenant Lane Brandon of the 21st Mississippi, learned from some Federal prisoners that the company attacking him, part of the 20th Massachusetts, was commanded by Lieutenant Henry Abbott, a former classmate of Brandon's at Harvard Law School. Brandon at once ordered his men to cease their withdrawal. According to a fellow officer, "He lost his head completely. He refused to retire before Abbott. He fought him fiercely and was actually driving him back. In this he was violating orders and breaking our plan of battle. He was put under arrest and his subaltern brought the command out of town."

Soon most of the Confederates had gained the protection of a stone wall at the foot of Marye's Heights. Private James Dinkins of the 18th Mississippi recalled that as Barks-

Confederate infantrymen defending
the town of Fredericksburg fight from
the cover of trees and houses against
Federals crossing the Rappahannock
(*background*) on December 11. The
17th and 18th Mississippi manned
this first defensive line, stalling the
Union attack for 12 hours.

dale's men withdrew from the burning city, "there was perfect order and steadiness, and the entire army was struck with it. As they emerged into the valley, a great cheer went up from Marye's Heights."

Although a few Confederate skirmishers remained behind in Fredericksburg, the town was now in Federal hands. A more aggressive commander might have attacked the heights immediately, but Burnside was in no hurry to move. "The Federals," Longstreet later observed dryly, "carefully matured their plans of advance and attack."

As night fell, flames licked away at sections of Fredericksburg. Thomas Galwey of the 8th Ohio, still on the east bank, described the scene: "The whole heavens are lit up by the burning city. On the heights beyond the city, for a mile or more, flashes of white light show through the smoke, as

the enemy's artillery seeks to demolish our bridges." The fire's glow, Galwey went on, "revealed skirmishers fighting in the streets, dodging about from house to house."

The following day, December 12, passed with Burnside doing nothing more than bringing more troops across the river and pondering his next move. The delay afforded the idle Federals a chance to indulge in one of the War's more discreditable enterprises — the wholesale looting of Fredericksburg.

The evacuation of most of the civilians and the withdrawal of the Confederates had left the town wide open. Most houses were empty, and many had been partially destroyed; the pickings were easy, and what the Federals could not use they demolished. They smashed mirrors, fine china and alabaster vases; mutilated books, paintings and embroidered draperies; and chopped up antique furniture for firewood. Rosewood pianos were piled in the streets and burned, or empolyed as horse troughs, or wrecked by soldiers who danced atop the instruments and kicked the keyboards apart. The streets filled with soldiers dressed in women's clothes and tall silk hats, and the sacking took on a bizarre, carnival-like quality. "It was ludicrous to see some men come along with large doll babies and children's toys, wigs on and white beavers and bonnets," wrote Private Alfred Davenport of the 5th New York. "But it made me feel sad to think how comfortable the homes were in time of peace now turned into desolation."

Major General Darius N. Couch, II Corps commander, was one of the few officers to take action to stop the looting. Couch placed guards at the bridges to make sure that none of the men got any of their loot back across the river to their camps. Huge piles of con-

In an improvised amphibious attack, men of the 7th Michigan and the 19th and 20th Massachusetts row pontoons across the river to Fredericksburg while engineers (*left*) work under fire to complete a bridge. A number of the engineers lie dead or wounded on the narrow bridge planking.

fiscated articles accumulated at the guard posts. But when the fighting broke out again, the booty mysteriously disappeared.

On the southern flank, downriver from Fredericksburg, the Federal advance under General Franklin was also stalled after a promising start on the morning of the 11th. Here Confederate opposition from the west bank had been far less effective than at the town. Two companies of 18th Mississippi opened fire on the Federal bridge-builders at dawn, wounding six men and shooting holes in many of the pontoons. But unlike the defenders at Fredericksburg, the Confederates

here had no buildings, walls and basements to protect them from artillery fire. When Federal gunners opened up, the Mississippians were quickly routed. "Twice afterwards, in much larger numbers, they attempted to rally," Major Magruder of the 15th New York Engineers recalled, "but were each time scattered in ludicrous confusion by the accurate fire of the batteries." One of the bridges was finished by 9 a.m., the other two hours later. But then they lay unused for several hours while General Franklin pondered the next move for his grand division.

William B. Franklin had graduated from West Point in 1843, at the top of the class in

Union soldiers engage in an orgy of looting on the night after capturing Fredericksburg. One witness observed a drunken but determined soldier carrying "a live goose by the leg in one hand and a black bottle by the neck in the other" as he pursued "a particularly lively pig up a street."

which Ulysses S. Grant had ranked 21st. Subsequently, Franklin had served as an engineer officer in various construction assignments around Washington, among them managing the erection of the new Capitol dome. Thus far in the War he had performed adequately at First Bull Run, in the Peninsular Campaign and at Antietam. But on the morning of December 11 he was hopelessly — if understandably — confused.

It was bad enough that the orders he received early that morning were vague in the extreme. "After your command has crossed," they read, "you will move down the Old Richmond Road, in the direction of the railroad, being governed by circumstances as to the extent of your movements." Perhaps in the hope of receiving a clarification, Franklin did not cross, but instead notified headquarters as soon as his bridges were ready. In reply, Burnside now instructed him not to cross, but to await further orders. Not until 4 p.m., about the time the Federals gained a foothold on the west bank at Fredericksburg, did Burnside order Franklin's grand division to move.

The first unit to cross the river was a brigade of VI Corps under Brigadier General Charles Devens Jr. One of Devens' regimental commanders decided that the occasion should be marked with proper ceremony, so he ordered a band to lead the way while playing a lively march. The men on the two spans picked up the cadence and fell into step — something that was never permitted on pontoon bridges lest the rhythmic tramp set up a dangerous swaying. Both bridges began to undulate alarmingly, but before any pontoons were swamped or moorings parted, a staff officer galloped up to the regimental commander and ordered the music stopped.

Devens' brigade and two regiments of another brigade that followed it soon reached the far bank, but then the advance was called to a halt; yet another order had arrived from Burnside that countermanded his preceding instructions. Now the fretful commanding general had decided that only one brigade of Franklin's grand division should deploy on the west bank, to guard the bridges during the night, and the rest of the troops should wait until morning. Back over the river plodded the two regiments, leaving Devens' brigade to hold the bridgehead. The following morning, Franklin's entire force crossed the Rappahannock, some of the men for the third time in less than 24 hours.

The grand division took up positions on the plain between the river and the heights held by the Confederates. Major General William F. Smith's VI Corps formed along the Old Richmond Road, which ran parallel to the river about a half mile inland. Smith's right was anchored on the steep bank of Deep Run. Major General John F. Reynolds deployed his I Corps on Smith's left in an arc stretching back to the Rappahannock. It was a situation that Smith found unsettling. As he later wrote: "Here were two corps with an impassable stream on their right, a formidable range of hills occupied by the enemy covering almost their entire front, and at their back a river with two frail bridges connecting its shores. It takes soldiers who do not believe that war is an art to be perfectly at ease under such circumstances."

By the time Franklin's dispositions were completed, more than 36 hours had passed since the engineers had begun laying the bridges, and Robert E. Lee had used the time to good advantage. During the night of December 11, Lee had ordered up two of

Stonewall Jackson's divisions. He brought A. P. Hill up from Yerby's House to relieve Longstreet's men on the Confederate right between Deep Run and Hamilton's Crossing. At the same time, General Taliaferro's troops moved up from Guinea Station to provide support. Lee left in place Jackson's other two divisions, under D. H. Hill and Jubal Early, to guard the crossings downstream at Skinker's Neck and Port Royal.

At midday on December 12, Lee rode out to reconnoiter the southern flank. He was joined by Stonewall Jackson and Major Heros Von Borcke, a Prussian officer serving on Jeb Stuart's staff. Reaching the heights beyond Deep Run, they entrusted their horses to an orderly and crept along a ditch to a point where they could see Franklin's troops deploying on the plain below. As the generals peered through their field glasses, Von Borcke thought nervously about what a well-directed shell or a few Federal horsemen could do at that moment to the leadership of the Army of Northern Virginia.

Von Borcke was relieved when they all returned to their horses and rode off. Lee was also relieved, but for another reason: His reconnaissance had erased any doubts about where the enemy was going to attack. Burnside was not going to make the wide flanking movement from Skinker's Neck after all, Lee concluded. Instead, the Federals were going to try to turn the Confederate right at Hamilton's Crossing, and the massing of troops on the plain suggested that an attack was imminent. Lee directed Jackson to summon the divisions of D. H. Hill and Jubal Early from their downstream positions.

Although the Federal plan of attack seemed clear to Lee and Jackson, General Franklin remained in the dark. He still had

Major General William B. Franklin, commander of the grand division on Burnside's left, failed to support the one promising Federal attack at Fredericksburg. Despite mediocre showings as a combat leader, he had risen steadily since the War's onset, from brigade commander to head of a division and then a corps.

no orders to engage the enemy, and his men stood idle in formation. He discussed matters with Generals Reynolds and Smith, and all three agreed that they should attack with their entire command to carry the ridge held by Jackson's troops and turn Lee's right.

At 5 p.m., Burnside rode out from his headquarters near Fredericksburg and made a cursory inspection of the southern flank. After his quick gallop along the lines, he was invited by Franklin to a meeting. There Franklin and his top generals pressed Burnside to approve an all-out attack.

Franklin would need time to reorganize his forces for such a large-scale assault, and he urged Burnside to approve the attack on the spot so that it could commence the following morning. Burnside demurred, but he left Franklin and his subordinates with the impression that orders authorizing the attack would be forthcoming.

Franklin and his generals prepared for the

At dawn on December 13, two Federal grand divisions, having crossed the Rappahannock, deployed for a frontal assault on the Confederate-held ridge west and south of Fredericksburg. In the town itself, General Edwin Sumner's Federal II and IX Corps assembled for an attack against General James Longstreet's forces, dug in along Marye's Heights. A mile to the south, William Franklin's I and VI Corps prepared to advance against Stonewall Jackson's corps. Jeb Stuart's cavalry secured the Confederate right flank, while the divisions of Jubal Early and D. H. Hill hastened from positions downriver to reinforce Jackson's troops.

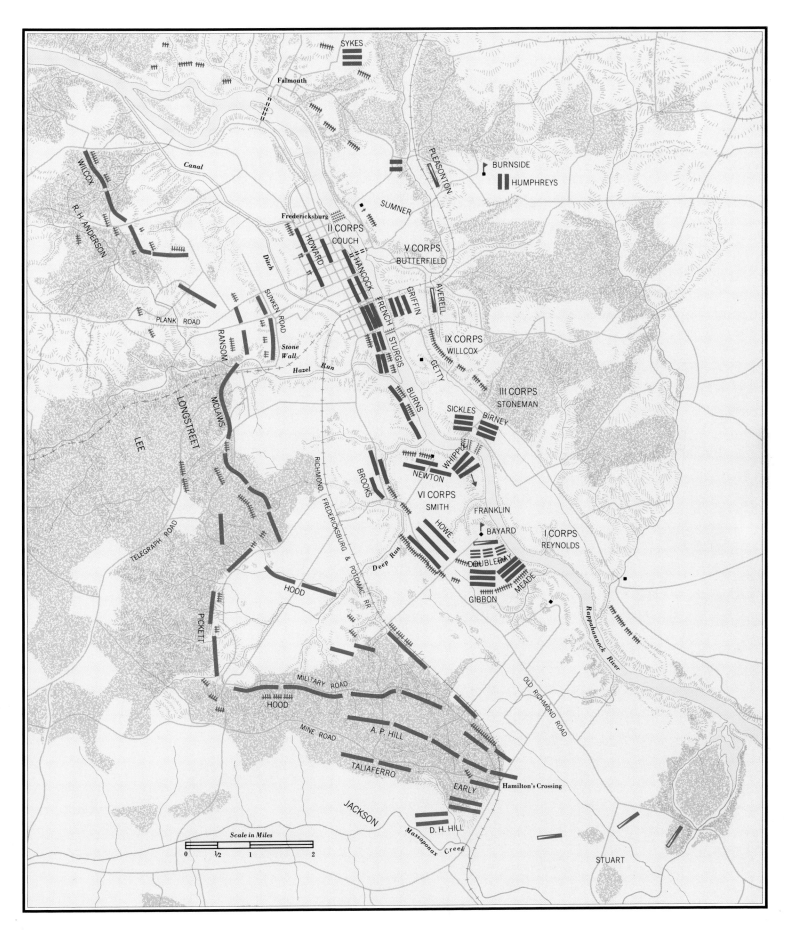

SYKES

Falmouth

Canal

WILLCOX

R. H. ANDERSON

PLEASONTON

SUMNER

BURNSIDE

HUMPHREYS

Fredericksburg

HOWARD

II CORPS
COUCH

V CORPS
BUTTERFIELD

Ditch

HANCOCK

PLANK ROAD

SUNKEN ROAD

RANSOM

FRENCH

GRIFFIN

AVERELL

Stone
Wall

Hazel Run

STURGIS

IX CORPS
WILLCOX

LONGSTREET

McLAWS

BURNS

GETTY

III CORPS
STONEMAN

LEE

SICKLES

BIRNEY

BROOKS

RICHMOND, FREDERICKSBURG & POTOMAC RR.

WHIPPLE

NEWTON

VI CORPS
SMITH

FRANKLIN

TELEGRAPH ROAD

HOWE

BAYARD

I CORPS
REYNOLDS

Rappahannock River

HOOD

Deep Run

DOUBLEDAY

MEADE

PICKETT

GIBBON

MILITARY ROAD

HOOD

MINE ROAD

A. P. HILL

OLD RICHMOND ROAD

TALIAFERRO

EARLY

Hamilton's Crossing

JACKSON

D. H. HILL

Massaponax Creek

STUART

Scale in Miles

0   ½   1   2

attack. But the night wore on with no word from Burnside. At 3 a.m., Reynolds gave up and went to bed, saying, "I know I have hard work ahead of me and I must get some sleep." Franklin then sent an aide to inquire at Burnside's headquarters. The aide was told that the orders would be ready promptly, but the hours dragged by without result.

General Smith was disgusted. He later wrote: "Burnside had persisted in crossing the river after all hope of a surprise had faded away, and now we must fight under great disadvantages." Smith still believed a concentrated assault could be successful, but wondered: "Would Burnside adopt our plan, and if so, why this delay which was costing us so much valuable time? We had all known Burnside socially, long and intimately, but in his new position of grave responsibility he was to us entirely unknown."

Stonewall Jackson's Sartorial Revival

While the Confederates prepared for battle at Fredericksburg, the men of Stonewall Jackson's corps witnessed an astonishing sight — their general inspecting the lines bedecked in a dazzling gold-braided uniform and a new forage cap to match (*below, right*). This splendid improvement over Jackson's customary threadbare attire drew catcalls and irreverent jests from his troops. "Old Jack will be afraid for his clothes," shouted one veteran in mock alarm, "and will not get down to work."

The new jacket had been given to Jackson by the always-elegant Jeb Stuart. The cap was a present from Jackson's wife, Anna. The general, according to an aide, "disliked exceedingly" his new headgear — apparently it did not fit properly — but he wore it for some months out of gallant regard for Mrs. Jackson's feelings.

Jackson's old cap (*below, left*), a relic of his days at the Virginia Military Institute, was supplanted by the smarter model with a wide gold band, bought by his wife from a shop in Richmond. Jackson's mapmaker, Jedediah Hotchkiss, was given the old cap as a souvenir.

The orders Franklin sorely needed were at last issued, at 5:55 a.m. But despite the availability of a telegraph, the directives were given to Brigadier General James A. Hardie of Burnside's staff to deliver personally. Hardie did not reach Franklin until 7:45.

Even worse, the orders were not at all what Franklin had expected. Instead of committing the entire grand division to the attack, Burnside directed cryptically that Franklin keep his command in position and send out "a division at least" to "seize, if possible, the height near Captain Hamilton's, on this side of the Massaponax, taking care to keep it well supported and its line of retreat open." Franklin had 60,000 men available, yet Burnside had given him no clear idea of how many of them he should commit. Left to his own devices, Franklin chose to interpret Burnside's order as cautiously as possible.

Months later, when Burnside was called before the Congressional Committee on the Conduct of the War to explain his thinking, he said only that he intended for Franklin to seize the heights above Hamilton's Crossing. Once Franklin's attack was under way, General Sumner's grand division, on the north flank at Fredericksburg, would assault Marye's Heights to prevent Longstreet's troops from going to Jackson's aid at the other end of the line. Whatever the merits of this strategy, the fact is that not one word of it was communicated to the Federal grand division commanders as they went into battle; they learned of it only when Burnside explained it to the Congressional committee.

What was worse, Burnside had seriously underestimated Confederate strength along the southern flank. He had made almost no effort to reconnoiter Lee's positions there or to keep watch on enemy movements. Early on the 13th he believed that "a large force of the enemy is concentrated near Port Royal, its left resting near Fredericksburg."

In fact, D. H. Hill's division had arrived in the Hamilton's Crossing area after a night's march from Port Royal, and Jubal Early's division had come up from Skinker's Neck. Jackson now had 30,000 men to defend his 3,000-yard-wide sector. A. P. Hill's division was in the front, backed up by the divisions of Jubal Early, D. H. Hill and William B. Taliaferro.

Jackson's troops were heavily supported by artillery. On the right, 14 guns were posted on Prospect Hill near Hamilton's Crossing; another 12 guns had been pushed out beyond the railroad track that ran along the bottom of the ridge; 21 more guns were in position on the left near Deep Run. And Jeb Stuart's cavalry division, deployed in an extended skirmish line on the extreme right and well out in front of the rest of Jackson's corps, had 18 guns under the command of the youthful Major John Pelham.

There was, however, a weak spot in A. P. Hill's line. When Hill deployed his troops along the forward slope of the ridge on the morning of December 12, he posted, from north to south, the brigades of Brigadier Generals William Dorsey Pender, James H. Lane and James J. Archer, then two regiments of Colonel John M. Brockenbrough's brigade. Between the brigades of Lane and Archer, there was a gap of 600 yards, approximately one fifth of Hill's entire front.

The gap was a heavily wooded area of swampy ground and tangled underbrush, in the form of a triangle. The point projected out beyond the railroad embankment at the base of the ridge for a third of a mile, almost halfway to the Old Richmond Road. Hill, assuming that this boggy area was impassable, left it undefended and thus allowed the enemy a covered approach to the heart of the Confederate positions. Above the unmanned area, in the woods along the crest of the ridge, Hill had posted Brigadier General Maxcy Gregg's South Carolina brigade.

Gregg was a scholarly lawyer who had served in the Mexican War, although he had seen no action. When South Carolina seceded in December 1860, he raised the 1st South Carolina Regiment, which included some of the state's outstanding citizens. After prov-

ing himself a lion-hearted combat leader at the Battles of Gaines's Mill, Second Bull Run and Antietam, he had been promoted to brigadier general.

Somehow, when his command was posted along the Military Road on the ridge above the undefended sector, Gregg failed to grasp that his was the only line of defense behind the gap. General Lane said later that he told Gregg about the undefended space to his front. But Gregg, who was slightly deaf, either did not hear or did not understand, and persisted in believing that the woods below

Men of Colonel J. M. Brockenbrough's 40th Virginia await the Federal attack on December 13 by a bend in the railroad near Hamilton's Crossing. These troops, supported by Colonel Robert L. Walker's artillery *(background)*, helped beat back the fierce Union assault through a gap in Stonewall Jackson's line.

him were held by Confederates. Moreover, he must have been thinking of a near-tragedy at Second Bull Run, when his brigade mistakenly fired on some of General Jubal Early's troops. No one had been hurt, but surely the experience was etched on Gregg's mind. At any rate, on the morning of December 13, he ordered his men to stack arms.

At 8:30 a.m. on the 13th, under the cover of morning fog, the Federals moved out to attack Jackson's positions. In the lead was Major General George Meade's Pennsylvania Reserve Division, supported on the right by Brigadier General John Gibbon's division; the left flank was guarded by Major General Abner Doubleday's division. After crossing a ravine and marching downriver parallel to the Rappahannock for about 800 yards, the attackers faced right, crossed the Old Richmond Road and formed a line of battle.

The Confederates were roughly a thousand yards away. For about half that distance the open plain rose slightly, then dipped into a gentle hollow that extended to the steep embankment of the railroad. On the other side of the tracks rose the wooded ridge where the Confederates waited. The only cover on the Federal side of the railroad was that inviting wedge of woods jutting out toward the right center of Meade's line.

The Confederates on the ridge could not see the force in front of them through the fog. But they could hear bands playing, the muffled sound of troops in motion, the rumble of guns and caissons, and the jingle of harnesses. Then at about 10 a.m. the fog lifted suddenly to reveal a spectacular scene — Franklin's entire grand division, stretching back to the river. "A slight but dazzling snow beneath, and a brillant sun above, in-

tensified the leaping reflections from fifty thousand gleaming bayonets," a Confederate soldier named J. H. Moore recalled. "Officers on restless horses rushed from point to point in gay uniforms. Field artillery was whisked into position as so many fragile toys. Rank and file, foot and horse, small arms and field ordnance presented so magnificent a pageant as to call forth the unbounded admiration of their adversaries."

One Confederate who watched with admiration — perhaps even a little envy — was General Longstreet. "I could see almost every soldier Franklin had," Longstreet wrote later, "and a splendid array it was. But off in the distance was Jackson's ragged infantry, and beyond was Stuart's battered cavalry, with their soiled hats and yellow butternut suits, a striking contrast to the handsomely equipped troops of the Federals."

Moore wrote that when the enemy troops settled down, "adjutants stepped to the front

and plainly in our view, read the orders of the day. This done, the fatal advance across the plain commenced." A regiment moved out in a skirmish line, followed by Meade's troops on the left and Gibbon's on the right. As they advanced, Moore wrote, Federal guns on the heights across the river "belched forth their missiles of destruction and swept the plain in advance of Franklin's columns, while at the same moment his smaller field-pieces in front and on the flanks joined in to sweep the open space on all sides."

Major John Pelham was watching Meade's preparations from the Confederate cavalry position below Hamilton's Crossing when he had a sudden inspiration. The aggressive young artilleryman asked General Stuart for permission to take two field guns down a country lane to its intersection with the Old Richmond Road and open a flanking fire at close range on the massed Federal troops. It was the kind of daring enterprise that appealed to Stuart, and he readily agreed. Pelham galloped off with two guns of Captain M. W. Henry's Virginia Artillery: a Blakely rifle and a 12-pounder Napoleon.

On reaching the Old Richmond Road, Pelham quickly unlimbered his guns and opened fire with solid shot on the densely massed troops. The little cannonade had a devastating effect; the lead Federal brigade faltered and came to a halt. Federal artillery-men quickly wheeled their pieces and directed a brutal fire on Pelham's position. The Blakely was disabled and had to be withdrawn. But Pelham's men redoubled their fire with the lone Napoleon, and by hitching up the gun and changing its position frequently, they managed to weather the bombardment. Realizing that their luck could not last, General Stuart sent word that Pelham should feel free to withdraw at any time, to which the young artilleryman responded, "Tell the General I can hold my ground."

Then Pelham was instructed three times to withdraw from his position. But not until his ammunition was almost exhausted did he come galloping back down the lane to rejoin Stuart's division. His bold action had cost the Federals dearly. A shot had mortally wounded the promising young cavalryman, Brigadier General George G. Bayard, as he rested in reserve near Franklin's headquarters, the Bernard House. More important, Pelham had stalled the Federal advance for more than half an hour.

With the artillery threat to his left gone, General Meade started the advance again,

Charging into ferocious Confederate fire, Pennsylvania infantrymen of Major General George Meade's division storm across the railroad embankment at the foot of the ridge on the south flank. "My men went in *beautifully*," Meade wrote shortly after the battle, "but finding themselves unsupported on either right or left, and encountering an overwhelming force of the enemy, they were checked and finally driven back."

leaving Doubleday in position to guard against Stuart's cavalry.

Except for Pelham's venture, Jackson's artillery had remained silent. But when the attackers were about 800 yards from the Confederate positions and still in the open, Colonel Robert L. Walker's guns on the ridge at the right end of the line, and Pelham's artillery down on the plain, opened fire. "Spaces, gaps and wide chasms instantly told the tale of a most fatal encounter," J. H. Moore recalled, as "volley after volley continued the work of destruction." The Federal line wavered and halted once again. A terrific artillery duel ensued. The Federal guns on the plains and on the heights across the river tried to silence the Confederate batteries and clear the wooded slopes of defend-

A West Point graduate and officer of engineers, George Gordon Meade vaulted from the rank of captain to brigadier general of volunteers when the Civil War began. Renowned for his intolerance of bungling subordinates, he was nicknamed "the Great Peppery" and "Old Snapping Turtle" by his aides.

ers, but Jackson's artillery continued to blast away at the stalled Federal lines.

During the worst of the bombardment, one Federal artillery commander, Captain James A. Hall of the 2nd Maine Battery, was sitting on his horse shouting over the din to two other officers while his men furiously served their guns. A shell came hurtling between Hall and the officers and struck a caisson nearby, exploding its ammunition with a blinding flash. Hall calmly dismounted, walked over to one of his guns, sighted it, signaled for the gun to be fired and watched for the shell to find its mark. Moments later, clearly visible in Hall's line of sight, a tremendous explosion on the enemy ridge sent up a geyser of shell fragments and flame. Satisfied with his work, the captain strolled back to his horse and remounted.

The artillery duel continued at a fever pitch until about 1 p.m., when the Federal gunners had to cease fire for fear of hitting their own troops, who were on the move again and nearing the Confederate-held ridge. One of the last shells fired by the Federals struck a Confederate caisson and set off a thunderous explosion that spread confusion among some of the defenders. Union troops raised a great cheer, and Meade seized the moment to order a charge.

In the lead, Meade's 1st Brigade pushed into the triangle of woods that had been left unmanned by the foe. The men mounted the railroad embankment, clawed their way uphill through the underbrush, then veered to the right — straight into the flank of Lane's Confederate brigade. Meade's 2nd Brigade, meanwhile, moved through the gap and turned left, slamming into Archer's flank. Expecting a frontal assault, the Confederates were astonished to see the Federals charging

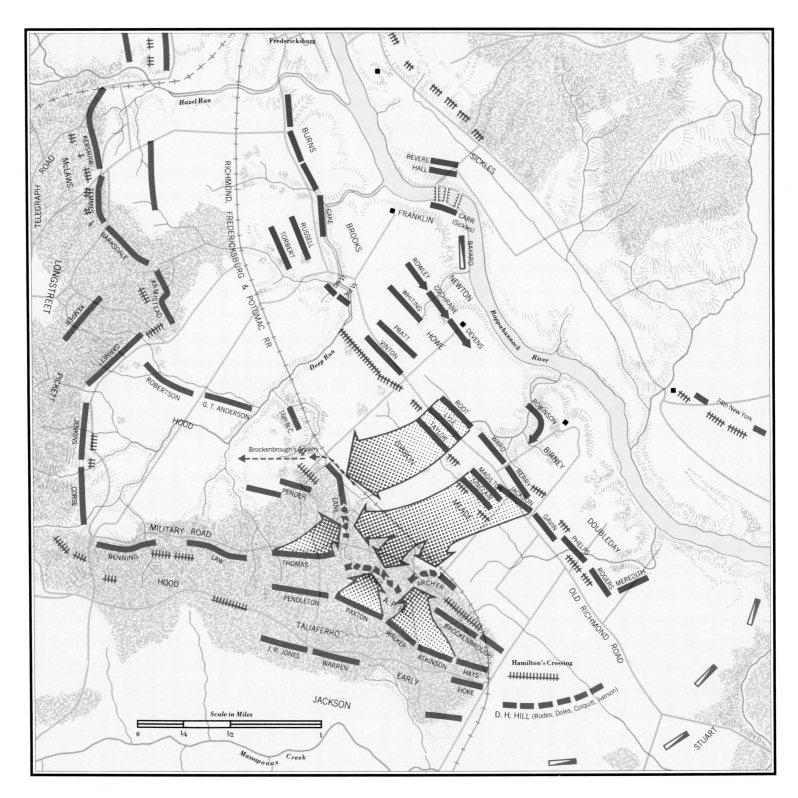

from woods thought impenetrable. Two of Archer's regiments, the 19th Georgia and 14th Tennessee, struggled to form a new line facing left, but were thrown back in disorder. Lane's men resisted fiercely, but they too had to fall back.

Thousands of Meade's men then poured into the widening gap between Lane's and Archer's brigades. Despite the dense brush, they surged up the hill to the crest, crossed the Military Road and stormed into General Gregg's position. Many of Gregg's men, still thinking that there were Confederates to their front, had taken cover from the shellfire, with their arms stacked nearby.

As the men of the 1st South Carolina Regiment leaped for their weapons, the befuddled Gregg dashed along the Military Road on his horse, shouting to them not to fire. Incredibly, he believed the attackers to be friendly troops. The Federals fell on the rows of stacked arms, and a wild scramble ensued. Many of the unarmed men of one Confederate unit, Orr's Rifles, were slaughtered; the remainder fled in disarray. Gregg, a heavy-set man in full general's uniform, was an easy target; he soon fell mortally wounded, a Minié ball through his spine. Meade's men swept over his command.

Then the tide shifted. Troops of Early's and Taliaferro's divisions, held in reserve behind Gregg's position, came rushing through the woods to meet the Federals head-on. Seeing this, the remaining regiments of Lane's and Archer's brigades rallied and managed to form new lines, facing the Federals in the gap. Meade's men now found themselves taking heavy fire from three sides. Lieutenant Daniel R. Coder's Company E of the 11th Pennsylvania Reserves was erased from the field. Of its 31 men, four were killed, 25

wounded, and one captured — only one man escaped unharmed. "We lost color bearer after color bearer," Coder recalled, "I picked up the colors three times myself. The flag staff was shot off and the flag perforated in 19 places by Rebel bullets."

Meade's 3rd Brigade, under the command of Brigadier General Conrad F. Jackson, now advanced into the maelstrom. Jackson's Federals came under heavy fire from a Confederate battery to their right and attempted to flank it, but Jackson was shot dead and his leaderless brigade was driven back.

On Meade's right, Gibbon's supporting attack had also bogged down. Deployed north of the wooded triangle, Gibbon's division had no cover to protect its advance to the railroad and the slope beyond, where Lane's well-protected Confederates waited among the trees. Gibbon attacked with his 3rd Brigade, then the 2nd, but both were stopped by concentrated artillery and small-arms fire and driven back in confusion. Gibbon then ordered Colonel Adrian Root's 1st Brigade across the tracks and over the treacherous open ground. Root's troops were soon slowed to a crawl by the devastating fire.

Lieutenant Abner Small, an aide to Colonel Root, saw a soldier trying to advance into the hurricane of artillery fire. The man could not make his legs support him. He fell to his knees and struggled in vain to rise, his face ashen and distorted. Small tried to shame him into moving by shouting "Coward!" The man screamed back, "You lie!" but still could not force himself to rise and go forward. After the attack, he came to Small in tears and said, "I couldn't go on, but I'm not a coward." Small, touched by the man's sincerity, asked his forgiveness.

On the field, Colonel Root and Brigadier

The 114th Pennsylvania Zouaves charge headlong
into a Confederate counterattack, helping to save
the Federal left from disaster after Meade's retreat.
Colonel Charles Collis, an Irish-born Philadelphian
who had raised the Zouave regiment, rides with the
colors among his troops, as his brigade commander, General John Robinson (*left foreground*), lies
pinned under his dead horse. Collis, then only 24,
received the Medal of Honor for this action.

General Nelson Taylor, commander of the 3rd Brigade, rode up and down the lines, urging the men forward into the withering fire. Somehow the officers managed to keep the advance moving. At length the Federals caught sight of enemy soldiers up ahead. A shout went up; the men leaped over ditches, surged over the railroad embankment and charged into the woods, striking into the heart of Lane's troops. In the hand-to-hand fighting that followed, the Federals initially prevailed and even managed to take 200 prisoners. But in the dense growth the attackers became disorganized, and Root rode back to ask General Gibbon for help and for further orders. Gibbon simply told him to press on.

Up above on the crest, the Confederate reserves commanded by Early were continuing their furious counterattack against Meade's troops, whose number had by this time been cut by more than a third. In the Federal rear, at least 20,000 men stood idle,

French Mary's Wartime Odyssey

Among the Union wounded at Fredericksburg was a slight woman known as "French Mary" Tepe (right), a civilian attached to Colonel Charles Collis' Zouave regiment. French Mary served as a vivandiere — a woman who carried tobacco and other luxuries to sell to the soldiers. What set French Mary apart from most other vivandieres serving with the Union Army was her courage on the battlefield and her devotion to her Zouaves. Between periods of fighting, she diligently washed and mended the men's torn and grimy clothes. During battles she often carried her small keg of whiskey to the front lines to comfort the wounded and encourage the faint of heart. Her bravery at Fredericksburg earned her a decoration from her corps.

The events of Mary Tepe's life are obscured in a haze of myth, but she seems to have been a French immigrant who married a Philadelphia tailor named Bernardo Tepe. When he enlisted in 1861, French Mary followed him to Virginia and, so legend has it, subsequently braved shot and shell at 13 battles in the East. Bernardo Tepe was taken prisoner in 1863; Mary later remarried, and after the War she ran a toy shop near Pittsburgh. The wound she suffered at Fredericksburg, a musket ball in the heel, continued to cause such pain, it is said, that it contributed to her suicide about 1900.

FRENCH MARY IN HER VIVANDIERE'S UNIFORM

but none were ordered to support the increasingly desperate attackers as the Confederate brigades swarmed down upon them. Perhaps Franklin was not sufficiently in touch with the battle and did not know that reserves were needed. Perhaps his judgment had been clouded by Burnside's indefinite and cautionary directive. At any rate, Meade's men, then Gibbon's, began to yield ground, and soon were driven back over the railroad embankment and out onto the plain.

Among the advancing Confederate units was one of Early's brigades, led by Colonel Robert Hoke. Hoke's men raced after the fleeing Federals and gained the railroad cut. Captain James Mishet later recalled that it was not empty of Federals: "I ran up in front of my men and jumped into the cut, landing on a big captain's head, ramming it down in the mud. The men piled in after us. A detail of three boys was made to show the prisoners where to go and they were ordered to get out quick to give us room."

The Confederate commanders had been ordered to pursue no farther than the railroad. Nevertheless, Hoke's brigade, along with that of Colonel Edmund N. Atkinson, forgot the limitation in the heat of the moment and chased the Federals almost to the Old Richmond Road. Only then did Franklin's reserve — the divisions of Brigadier General David Birney and Major General Daniel Sickles — get the order to move into action. The audacious band of Confederates tore into two regiments of Birney's troops, inflicting hundreds of casualties; for a moment it looked as though the Confederate spearhead would drive all the way to the river. But the grayclads were short of ammunition and unsupported, and before long they ran into concentrated canister fire from 18 guns under Captain George E. Randolph. Now disorganized, the Confederates withdrew to the wooded ridge, leaving Colonel Atkinson among those wounded in the field.

Less than two hours after the first Federal infantry assault, both sides were back where they started. Franklin's divisions had lost 4,830 men, with nothing to show for it but a few hundred prisoners. Jackson's losses were also severe — 3,415 from a force of 30,000 men — but he was more than ready to continue the contest. In fact, later that afternoon, when Franklin re-formed his lines but sent out nothing more than skirmishers, Jackson decided to launch a counterattack and ordered a preliminary movement by the artillery. But the movement provoked a furious response from the Federal gunners, and seeing that daylight was waning, Jackson reluctantly called off the assault.

Earlier, at 2:30 p.m., after the Federals had been driven back to the Old Richmond Road, Burnside had abruptly asserted his authority with an order to Franklin to renew the attack. But many of Franklin's officers were by then utterly disheartened. They had believed the assault to be hopeless from the outset; they had nevertheless punctured the Confederate line, only to see the advantage lost — along with thousands of lives. Many were furious with Franklin for not properly supporting Meade's attack. Franklin, for his part, was demoralized. He had lost all faith in Burnside, and he proceeded to ignore the order to send his men back into battle. In so doing, he avoided the wholesale slaughter that was at that moment being visited on the hapless men of General Sumner's command at the foot of Marye's Heights.

The Debacle on Marye's Heights

"The slaughter is terrible — the result disastrous. Until we have good generals it is useless to fight battles."

LIEUTENANT HENRY H. CURRAN, 146TH NEW YORK, AFTER THE BATTLE OF FREDERICKSBURG

In Fredericksburg, on the morning of December 13, Private Eugene Cory of the 4th New York Infantry had been awakened from a fitful sleep on the floor of a mansion by the frightening crash of artillery shells. The Confederate guns on the heights to the west had begun dropping shells into the fog-cloaked city in hopes of doing some damage to the Federal troops presumably forming in the streets. The result, Cory recalled, was "perfect pandemonium," with shells screaming overhead and bursting among the houses; brick and metal fragments flew about, killing and maiming horses and men.

Despite the shelling, the 4th New York, along with the other troops of General Darius N. Couch's II Corps, stood in columns in the streets and awaited the order to advance. Standing there under the bombardment was, in Cory's words, "perhaps the most trying position in which a soldier can be placed," imposing as it did all the danger and terror of war without the "exhilaration and excitement of action." Cory and the other men looked forward to the order to move out; they would be marching into a hot fire, they knew, but anything was better than waiting helplessly under the exploding shells.

Cory's regiment was part of Brigadier General William H. French's division, which had been selected to head the Federal attack on the north flank. Burnside's orders to the grand division commander, General Sumner, instructed him to send "a

division or more" to seize the high ground beyond the town.

Although Sumner craved action, he would not personally lead this assault. His habit of taking his men into battle was popular with the troops, but was regarded by his superior as excessively rash for a grand division commander; Burnside had ordered Sumner not to cross the river. Thus, on the north flank, the two highest-ranking Federal generals — Burnside and Sumner — would be separated by the Rappahannock from the field of combat. And their isolation would crucially affect the outcome of the battle.

Once the fog lifted and the order came to advance, the men would have to march through the town on streets leading westward toward the Confederate positions in the hills. The nearest of these was Marye's Heights, a low ridge about 600 yards outside Fredericksburg.

The intervening plain was mostly flat and open, but presented a number of obstacles to men advancing under heavy artillery fire. A few scattered houses offered some shelter, but the surrounding gardens and fences would only slow the troops. About 200 yards from the edge of town lay a canal, spanned by three narrow bridges; the men would have to form columns and file across the bridges under the very muzzles of the Confederate cannon. Worse, the planking had been torn up from one of these spans, and the advancing troops would have to pick their way across on the stringers.

Sergeant Thomas Plunkett of the 21st Massachusetts stands proudly by the regimental colors he carried in the doomed Federal attack on Marye's Heights. A direct hit by a Confederate shell cost Plunkett one of his arms and part of the other, and stained the flag with his blood, but he survived, and was awarded the Medal of Honor for his courage.

On the far side of the canal, a low bluff offered some cover, and about 350 yards beyond the bluff there was a slight incline, where men could get out of the direct line of Confederate fire by lying flat and hugging the ground. But elsewhere on the field, there was virtually no protection at all.

The Federal soldiers could see the enemy guns and troops looming on the heights, but they could only discern the outline of the closest Confederate position — a lane running along the foot of the ridge. Later known simply as the Sunken Road, the lane was protected on its forward edge by a stone wall four feet high. The Confederates had dug a ditch just behind the wall, packing the scooped-out earth against the stones on the exposed side for added protection and concealment. It was a nearly perfect defensive position; troops standing in the Sunken Road could fire comfortably across the shoulder-high wall with minimum exposure to enemy rounds.

The Confederate division commander on Marye's Heights, Lafayette McLaws, had deployed Brigadier General Thomas Cobb's Georgia brigade in the Sunken Road, and had stationed the 24th North Carolina, under Brigadier General Robert Ransom, in trenches that extended the line northward 250 yards from the point where the wall ended. McLaws had 2,000 men on the line, with an additional 7,000 troops in reserve behind the ridge. The Georgians were positioned behind the stone wall in two ranks; one rank was to fire, then step to the rear to reload while the other was firing.

In addition, the Confederate infantrymen were strongly supported by artillery massed on the ridge above them. The approaches to Marye's Heights had been so thoroughly covered that when the corps commander, General Longstreet, spotted an idle gun and suggested that it be pressed into service, his artillery chief, Colonel E. Porter Alexander, casually dismissed his superior's concern. "General," he said, "we cover that ground now so well that we will comb it as with a fine-tooth comb. A chicken could not live on that field when we open on it."

The fog lifted about 10 a.m., and an hour later Sumner gave the order to advance. French's division, led by Brigadier General

Nathan Kimball's brigade, moved out shortly before noon. The men started off in a tightly packed column dictated by the need to cross the canal bridges, and the moment they emerged from the cover of the town their dense formation came under murderous artillery fire; a single shell killed or wounded 18 men in the 88th New York.

But the troops closed up and pressed forward, trotting across one of the canal bridges toward the protective cover of the bluff on the far side.

There the division formed a line of battle and, before advancing on the heights, fixed bayonets. "The clink, clink, clink of the cold steel," recalled a Federal private, "made

In a view toward Marye's Heights, the open ground on the southwest edge of Fredericksburg — site of the Federals' so-called "march of death" — lies desolate in this panoramic photograph taken 17 months after the battle. At right, along Hanover Street, are the battered houses that provided momentary cover for the advancing Federals.

one's blood run cold." At the bluff the adjutant of the 132nd Pennsylvania, Lieutenant Frederick L. Hitchcock, discovered that in the noise and confusion of the bombardment nine of his regiment's 10 companies had been held up in the city, and realized that he must go back through the rain of Confederate shellfire and get them. "In that moment," he wrote later, "I gave my life up. The nervous strain was simply awful. The atmosphere seemed surcharged with the most startling and frightful things. Deaths, wounds, and appalling destruction everywhere."

As Hitchcock made the mad dash rearward, he glimpsed three men headed back dragging a bleeding man whose leg had been

severed and was hanging by a tendon. The rescuers, Hitchcock wrote, were "jumping and dodging at every shell that exploded, jerking and twisting this dangling leg to his horrible torture. I remember hearing him beseeching them to lay him down and let him die. They were probably a trio of cowards trying to get back from the front."

Hitchcock found the rest of his regiment and summoned the courage to lead the men across the canal to the bluff. But as he said years later, "I can fully appreciate the story of the soldier's soliloquy as he saw a rabbit sprinting back from the line of fire: 'Go it, cotton tail; if I hadn't a reputation at stake, I'd go too.' "

In spite of the bombardment, General French's brigades advanced up the hill from the bluff in perfect line of battle. "How beautifully they came on!" remembered a watching Confederate, Lieutenant William M. Owen of the Washington Artillery of New Orleans. "Their bright bayonets glistening in the sunlight made the line look like a huge serpent of blue and steel. The very force of their onset leveled the broad fences bounding the small fields and gardens that interspersed the plain. We could see our

As seen from behind the Federal lines, regiments of Brigadier General Nathan Kimball's brigade lead the assault on Marye's Heights (*background*) at noon on December 13. At far left the men of the 4th and 8th Ohio fire while lying prone on a slight slope. The 24th New Jersey advances in the center amid exploding artillery shells, and the 28th New Jersey moves forward on the right.

shells bursting in their ranks, making great gaps. But on they came, as though they would go straight through and over us."

Kimball's brigade, already cut up by the artillery fire, slogged grimly up the muddy slope until it was within 125 yards of the Confederate line. Suddenly a sheet of flame flared from behind the stone wall. Another Confederate volley followed quickly, then another and another. Hundreds of Federal soldiers fell dead or wounded in that awful, almost-continuous storm of lead. A few men made their way — firing, reloading and resuming their advance — to within 40 yards of the wall, and a few others ran for cover among some houses nearby, but most reeled back before the searing blasts and fell prone behind the incline, seeking cover from which to fire on the Confederate line. Within 20 minutes, a quarter of Kimball's brigade had been put out of action. Kimball himself was severely wounded in the thigh and had to be carried off the field.

French's 3rd Brigade, under Colonel John W. Andrews, followed Kimball's men into action. In that formation was the 4th New York's Private Cory; the events of the next few minutes would be permanently etched in his memory. The men marched up the hill shoulder to shoulder, with compressed lips and shortened breath, "the very air lurid, and alive with the flashes of guns, and rent with the long shriek of solid shot and shell, and the wicked whistle of grape."

They reached the top of the incline and faced the concentrated fire of the Georgians. "Here almost blown off our feet, staggering as though against a mighty wind, the line for a few minutes held its ground," Cory recalled, "then slowly and sullenly it gave way, and retiring a few paces below the brow of the hill, there lay down, panting for breath, and clinging to the ground so desperately attained."

In a little more than 15 minutes, nearly half of Andrews' brigade had been killed or wounded. Following closely at the double-quick, Colonel Oliver H. Palmer's brigade got no closer to the Sunken Road and suffered similarly devastating losses. French's division had been shot to pieces. Now it was the turn of Major General Winfield Scott Hancock, whose division had been ordered to follow in support of French.

Hancock rode out with his staff — "as cool and brave as a lion," a fellow officer observed — giving directions and urging his men to the attack. Colonel Samuel K. Zook's brigade charged up the hill with speed and determination. But, as one of Zook's staff officers recalled, "the losses were so tremendous that before we knew it, our momentum was gone, and the charge a failure." The survivors fell back to the incline, which was now heaped with a grisly tangle of the dead, the wounded and the desperate.

Next came Brigadier General Thomas Francis Meagher's Irish Brigade. The men, advancing at the double-quick, carried a green flag and wore green sprigs in their caps to celebrate their heritage. By chance, they faced a sector of the Confederate line held by the Irishmen of Colonel Robert McMillan's 24th Georgia Regiment. The Confederates recognized their countrymen by their green emblems, and someone exclaimed, "What a pity. Here come Meagher's fellows." Then the Georgians took aim and mowed their fellow Irishmen down.

The last of Hancock's brigades to go into action was that of Brigadier General John Caldwell. As Caldwell's troops advanced, the two regiments on the left, commanded by 23-year-old Colonel Nelson A. Miles, were ordered to shift to the right. Miles marched his men laterally through the withering fire, and then forward to within 40 yards of the stone wall. Then they too were driven back with terrible losses.

The repulse convinced Colonel Miles that the Federal tactics were dead wrong. Against the awesome strength of the Confederate position, the infantrymen had been ordered to advance in the conventional manner, stopping at intervals to fire, reloading and then moving on. As they paused in the open, they made perfect stationary targets for the Confederates. The adjutant of the 132nd Pennsylvania, Lieutenant Hitchcock, who was severely wounded in front of the stone wall, later summed up the futility of this approach: "It was like standing upon a raised platform to be shot down by those sheltered behind it. Had we been ordered to fix bayonets and charge those heights we could have understood the movement, though that would have been an impossible undertaking, defended as they were. But to be sent close up to those lines to maintain a firing line without any intrenchments or other

Brigadier General Thomas R. R. Cobb (*right*), a Georgian who was killed commanding the Confederate defenders at the stone wall, was a respected legal scholar and an early advocate of secession. With his older brother Howell, a former governor of Georgia who also became a general, Cobb had been instrumental in leading his state out of the Union.

Protected by a chest-high wall of stone, two ranks of Confederate infantrymen alternately step up to fire and move back to reload in the Sunken Road at the foot of Marye's Heights. General Longstreet wrote later that the Federals before the wall "fell like the steady dripping of rain from the eaves of a house."

shelter, if that was its purpose, was to simply invite wholesale slaughter without the least compensation."

Colonel Miles believed that a bayonet charge would at least give the men a fighting chance — and just might succeed if it involved great numbers, overwhelming the Confederates with sheer mass and momentum. He offered to make such a concentrated bayonet charge, but Caldwell denied permission. "It seemed to me a wanton loss of brave men," the general explained later.

While awaiting Caldwell's answer, Miles received a terrible wound: A bullet caught him in the throat and came out behind his left ear. "His comrades expected him to die at any time," recalled Major General Oliver O. Howard, whose division was waiting behind Hancock's. But Miles remained conscious and full of fight, and took his case for a bayonet charge back to Howard. As the general remembered what transpired, Miles gripped his bleeding throat, "holding together the lacerated pieces of flesh with his hands. He staggered to my headquarters, delivered his message and then fainted away. He was determined either to be killed or promoted."

Along the front, the slaughter continued. The 5th New Hampshire, under Colonel Edward E. Cross, was on the right flank of Caldwell's line. Twice wounded earlier in the War, Cross had had a premonition that this would be his last battle. Before going into action he had made his will, inventoried his property, packed everything he owned into a trunk, locked it and given the key to the regimental chaplain.

As the New Hampshire men charged up the slope, a shell exploded directly in front of Cross, at eye level. Fragments struck him in the face, the chest and one hand, and the blast smashed him to the ground. He lay there unconscious for a few moments until he was aroused by a blow to one leg. Struggling to his hands and knees, he spat out blood, sand, stones and two teeth. Trying to get to his feet, he collapsed again as shells burst all around him. A fragment struck the scabbard of his sword with such force that it rolled him over. He lay still and awaited death, counting grimly to keep from losing his mind.

As the battle raged around him, Cross was trampled repeatedly by troops charging to the front and others running to the rear. Three hours passed before Cross was discovered by one of his men, and not until dark could he be taken from the field to one of the houses in town that served as a hospital—in his case the mayor's home. While he was being carried in, he heard someone ask what had become of Colonel Cross. When a voice replied, "He is dead," the colonel raised his head and snapped, "Not by a damned sight."

When the carnage had continued for an hour, General Couch, the II Corps commander, came to the same conclusion that Colonel Miles had reached earlier: The impregnability of the stone wall to advancing riflemen required a change of tactics. Couch sent word to Generals French and Hancock to carry the enemy works by storm; if the Confederates could not be shot out of their position, perhaps they could be driven out by overwhelming numbers and cold steel. Then Couch climbed to the steeple of the city's courthouse to get above the smoke and haze and survey the field.

He was appalled at the sight. "Oh! Great God! See how our men, our poor fellows are

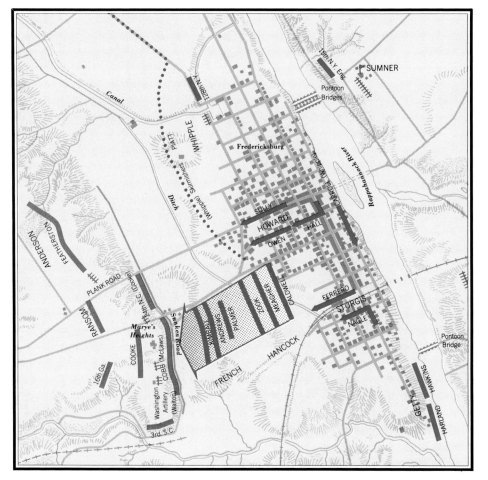

falling!" he exclaimed. The entire plain was covered with the wreckage of battle: dead men and horses, blueclad soldiers falling before the enemy fire, men running about aimlessly, the wounded streaming back from the battlefield. "There was no cheering on the part of the men," Couch remembered, "but a stubborn determination to obey orders and do their duty. I don't think there was much feeling of success."

Couch watched fresh units come up the hill. "As they charged, the artillery fire would break their formation and they would get mixed; then they would close up, go forward, receive the withering infantry fire, and

Shortly before noon on December 13 at Fredericksburg, William French's division led the Federal advance west from the town, with Winfield Scott Hancock's division close behind. Confederate batteries on Marye's Heights slowed the Federal assault. Then volleys of musketry from Thomas Cobb's brigade, behind the stone wall, and from John R. Cooke's brigade, atop the heights, decimated the Federal line.

Field glasses in hand, General Robert E. Lee, accompanied by General Longstreet (*second from right*) and several aides, watches the Confederate victory unfold from a hilltop near the lines. "It is well war is so frightful," Lee told his officers as he observed the action. "Otherwise we should become too fond of it."

those who were able would run to the houses and fight as best they could; and then the next brigade coming up in succession would do its duty and melt like snow coming down on warm ground." From Couch's vantage point, it was obvious that French's and Hancock's troops were so badly mauled that they could never mount a bayonet charge. In fact, the futility of all frontal attacks was evident

to him. "It is only murder now," he said.

Committing his last division, Couch determined to try yet another tactic. He ordered General Howard to try to work two brigades around to the right of French's and Hancock's men to turn the Confederate left. But before the order could be executed, both French and Hancock issued desperate calls for reinforcements at the center of the line, and Howard's division had to be sent to their aid. His men advanced over and around the troops felled in the earlier assaults. "The grass was slippery with their blood," recalled a soldier of the 19th Massachusetts. "Their ghastly lips seemed to appeal for vengeance." Colonel Joshua Owen took his brigade up the hill and reported back to Howard: "I was sent out here to support General Hancock's division, but there is not much left of it to support." Hancock's division had, in fact, lost 2,049 men — 42 per cent of its strength — the greatest divisional loss in any battle of the War.

Owen ordered his men to lie down and fire only when they saw a target. Then he called for reinforcements. The brigade under Colonel Norman J. Hall and two regiments of Brigadier General Alfred Sully's brigade moved up in support, but they could make no headway.

Next a IX Corps division under Brigadier General Samuel Sturgis was thrown in. Sturgis sent a brigade to attack on the left. When this brigade was pinned down, he ordered up another to assist it. "My entire division was now engaged," Sturgis wrote, "and every effort was made that could be made to carry the rifle-pits and stone fence of the enemy, but without success. Every man fought as if the fate of the day depended upon his own individual exertion."

Charge of the Irish Brigade

Thomas Francis Meagher, the commander of the Irish Brigade, urged his fellow immigrants to fight "today to preserve America, tomorrow to liberate Ireland." He had been a leader of the failed Irish rebellion of 1848.

A golden sunburst over Erin's harp and a bank of shamrocks decorate the flag carried at Fredericksburg by the 28th Massachusetts of the Irish Brigade. Written in Gaelic on the streamer is "Clear the way!"

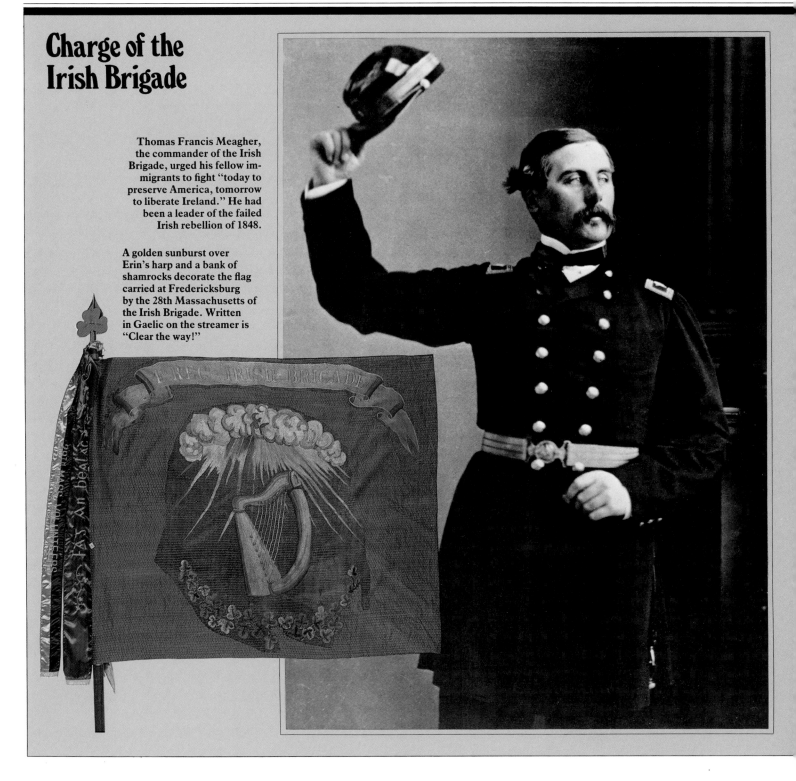

Few men fought with such wild abandon as the Irish Brigade. These troops, regiments of volunteers from New York City, Boston and Philadelphia, were among the two million Irish immigrants who had fled famine and English oppression in the 20 years before the Civil War. They were brawny canal diggers, track layers, hod carriers and bartenders, leavened by a smattering of lawyers, teachers, writers and merchants. They fought for their new country, both to earn acceptance as citizens and to train for the conflict they dreamed of — the war to liberate Ireland.

Their general, Thomas Meagher, was a swashbuckling Irish exile, Jesuit-educated and an impassioned orator. Known as "Meagher of the Sword," he had led his troops to glory at Frayser's Farm, Malvern Hill and Antietam's Bloody Lane.

Between battles, Meagher presided over the most convivial camp in the Army, a bivouac alive with songfests and horse races. There was even a tavern that flourished despite the Temperance Society formed by one determined brigade chaplain.

On the morning of December 13, 1862, the brigade took its place in Hancock's division and charged Marye's Heights in the second wave. A Federal officer pinned down on the slope watched the Irishmen advance and later re-created the scene. The men marched out from town, he wrote, "in glorious style, their green sunbursts waving. Every man has a sprig of green in his cap, and a half-laughing half-murderous look in his eye. They pass just to our left, poor glorious fellows, shaking goodbye to us with their hats. They reach a point within a stone's throw of the stone wall. They try to go beyond, but are slaughtered. Nothing could advance further and live."

Of the 1,300 men who attacked under the Irish Brigade's green and gold banners, by nightfall 545 were killed, wounded or missing, presumed dead.

Among five members of the Irish Brigade, photographed at their Virginia campsite in 1862, are Catholic chaplains James Dillon and William Corby (*seated center and right*). Father Corby went on to become president of Notre Dame University.

Four divisions had now tried to carry the position that Burnside had expected to seize with "a division or more," and all had been repulsed with heavy losses. After two hours of fruitless slaughter, the Federals paused to re-form their shattered units.

On the other side of the stone wall, the Confederates remained supremely confident. The tone of self-assurance had been set by General Cobb before the battle began. Longstreet had been worried about what might happen to Cobb's brigade at the stone wall if the weaker line to the north should be forced to withdraw; he had sent an urgent message to Cobb to fall back in the event that the Federals turned the left flank. But a movement to the rear was the farthest thing from Cobb's mind. "Well! If they wait for me to fall back," he told an aide, "they will wait a long time."

Observing the battle from a nearby hill, Robert E. Lee at one point also expressed some concern. And now it was Longstreet who offered reassurance. Having watched wave after wave of attackers come up the incline, Lee saw the Federals re-forming for new attempts, and remarked to Longstreet: "General, they are massing very heavily and will break your line, I am afraid." Longstreet's reply was serene: "General, if you put every man on the other side of the Potomac on that field to approach me over the same line, and give me plenty of ammunition, I will kill them all before they reach my line."

Nevertheless, Longstreet prudently hedged his bets. He had Brigadier General Joseph Kershaw move two regiments down from the ridge, and they joined Cobb's Georgians in the Sunken Road just as two rein-

forcing regiments sent by General Ransom arrived there. Cobb was deploying his men to meet the renewed assault when he suddenly gasped and fell to the ground. A sharpshooter's bullet had struck him in the thigh, severing an artery. Stretcher-bearers rushed him to a small house nearby, where a surgeon tried in vain to stop the bleeding. Within minutes, General Cobb was dead.

General Kershaw took command at the stone wall. With his reinforcements in the line, he now had four ranks of infantry behind the wall, capable of generating a concentrated firepower that Kershaw would describe as "the most rapid and continuous that I have ever witnessed."

By early afternoon the Federal lines facing Longstreet on the north and Jackson on the south had fallen back with heavy casualties.

From an impregnable position along Marye's Heights, Confederate infantrymen, supported by the elite Washington Artillery of New Orleans (*right, rear*), fire into dense lines of Federals struggling up the slope. The battlefield artist, an English journalist, made note of a shallow ravine where some Federals took cover.

reported later, "that it would be a useless waste of life to attack with the force at my disposal." And he went back across the river to advise Burnside not to attack.

During Hooker's absence, his V Corps commander, Brigadier General Daniel Butterfield, ordered Brigadier General Charles Griffin's 1st Division onto the field to relieve Sturgis' troops on the left. Griffin brought up his three brigades and sent them, one by one, against the Confederate position.

General Couch, watching the battle, could see Sturgis' troops being cut down, and he determined to send a battery forward onto the plain to shell the Confederate line. Couch's chief of artillery, Captain Charles Morgan, reacted with dismay. "General, a battery can't live there," he protested. But Couch's response was unyielding: "Then it must die there."

Captain John G. Hazard of the 1st Rhode Island Light Artillery was ordered to take the six guns of Battery B across the canal, place them in a position only 150 yards from the stone wall and open fire on the entrenched Confederates. Hazard's men came under heavy fire from sharpshooters and cannon the moment they began the gallop forward with their 12-pounders. Many of the horses and men were shot down before the guns could even be unlimbered. The crews did manage to open fire, but for all their gallantry were unable to affect the outcome. The Federal troops remained pinned down.

Meanwhile, someone in Hancock's battered division spotted troop movements on Marye's Heights and jumped to the erroneous conclusion that the Confederates were retreating. Dubious or not, the Federal command could not allow the opportunity to pass. It was the unhappy lot of Brigadier

The Army of the Potomac, its organization and will to fight rapidly disintegrating, desperately needed a fresh approach, but General Burnside's stubborn streak reasserted itself. It had taken him the better part of a month to decide how to fight this battle, and now that he had committed himself he could neither give up nor change his course; he simply ordered Franklin to renew his attack on Jackson — this the order that Franklin ignored — and directed Hooker, who was holding his grand division in reserve, to cross the Rappahannock and put everything he had into a renewed attack on Marye's Heights.

While his troops were crossing the river, General Hooker did what Burnside had yet to do; he rode onto the battlefield, conferred with officers on the scene, and assessed the situation. Hooker was soon convinced, he

At dusk outside Fredericksburg on the 13th, Thomas Cobb's brigade, now reinforced and led by Joseph Kershaw, still held the stone wall, supported by fresh Confederate artillery. On the plain below, Joseph Hooker launched a final assault: Andrew Humphreys' brigades charged along Hanover Street, while Charles Griffin attacked the center in three waves. On the left the lead brigade of George Getty's division pushed close to the wall's south end. But all the attacks were repulsed.

General Andrew Humphreys, leading the 3rd Division of V Corps, to attack next. "After an interval of more than 25 years," wrote General Couch, "I well recollect the grim determination which settled on the face of that gallant hero when he received the words, 'Now is the time for you to go in.'"

Calmly, Humphreys turned to his staff (which included his son, Lieutenant Henry H. Humphreys) and said, "Gentlemen, I shall lead the charge. I presume, of course, you will wish to ride with me." Then he led his 2nd Brigade in yet another gallant advance across the same bloody ground. They had no more success than the units that had preceded them, and Humphreys, like Miles and Couch before him, realized that nothing could be accomplished so long as the men continued to stop in order to take aim and fire at the Confederates.

Returning to where his 1st Brigade stood waiting their turn to attack, Humphreys ordered his men not to load their rifles, but to fix bayonets and charge right over the masses of men prostrate on the little incline. Then he galloped his black horse along the lines shouting, "Officers to the front in this charge. Never mind the obstacles in the way! Charge!" And once again he led the way into the storm of artillery and musket fire. The Federals lying wounded on the ground called out to the attackers, "Halt! Lie down — you will all be killed," and some of them even reached up to clutch at the advancing troops to stop them. The brigade became disorganized.

A Confederate infantryman who waited for Humphreys' troops to approach recalled, "They were allowed to come within 50 yards. Then our quintuple line rose up from behind the stone wall and delivered their

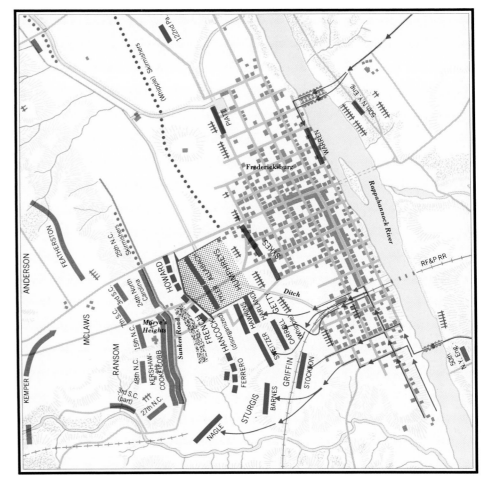

withering fire. The first line melted, but the second came steadily on, over the dead and dying of the former charges, to share the same fate. Ye Gods! It is no longer a battle, it is a butchery!"

With another 1,000 men dead or wounded since the fighting had been renewed, the Federal line fell back again, despite the efforts of Humphreys and other officers to hold it. Brigadier General George Sykes's division of Regular Army troops was ordered to cover Humphreys' retreat. Sykes's men had scarcely been deployed before they, too, were caught in the Confederate fire storm. Just as Griffin's men had done on

In midbattle, Major General Joseph Hooker (*left*) urges Burnside to halt the ruinous assaults on Marye's Heights, visible in the distance. But Burnside, gesturing toward the field, stubbornly orders Hooker to attack.

Hooker ordered Brigadier General George W. Getty's IX Corps division to launch an assault against the Confederate position on the left, at the foot of the section of Marye's Heights known as Willis's Hill. Colonel Rush Hawkins' brigade drew the onerous duty. For a time the Confederates did not detect Hawkins' troops advancing in the twilight, but that only delayed the inevitable. When the defenders did open fire, they shattered and repulsed Hawkins' men as they had all the others.

Hooker ordered an end to the fighting for the day; later he observed that he had "lost as many men as his orders required." Seven divisions had now been hurled against the enemy position on Marye's Heights, at a cost of about 7,000 casualties; the Confederates there had lost only 1,200 men, and they had allowed not a single Federal soldier to reach the stone wall. Federal burial parties reported that Zook's 53rd Pennsylvania, Meagher's 69th New York and Caldwell's 5th New Hampshire shared the sad honor of having left their dead closest to the objective.

When Sumner's and Hooker's casualties were added to Franklin's losses down the river, the Federal toll came to 12,535 killed or wounded, compared with total Confederate losses of about 5,000. The statistics confirmed General Longstreet's crisp assessment of the Federal performance that day: "The charges had been desperate and bloody, but utterly hopeless."

the right, Sykes's troops found what cover they could on the open plain and remained there under fire.

Hooker had returned at last from his fruitless meeting with Burnside; the commanding general had rebuffed Hooker's objections and demanded that the attacks continue. Although the day was fast waning,

Bitter cold descended on the plain that night. Some of the Federal troops had been ordered to hold their position, and other units remained pinned to the ground for fear of enemy fire. The thousands of wounded still lying on the field suffered appallingly. They cried out for help, for water, for their mothers, and for death.

Lieutenant Colonel Joshua Chamberlain, whose 20th Maine Regiment was pinned down before the stone wall, later described what he heard that night as "a smothered moan that seemed to come from distances beyond reach of the natural senses, as if a thousand discords were flowing together in a keynote weird, unearthly, terrible to hear and bear, yet startling with its nearness; some with delirious dreamy voices murmuring loved names, as if the dearest were bending over them; and underneath, all the time, that deep bass note from closed lips too hopeless or too heroic to articulate their agony."

As wounded men died, their bodies quickly froze, and many were stacked up to form barriers against the biting wind for those who still lived. Colonel Chamberlain slept between two such corpses for shelter, drawing a third crosswise to serve as a pillow and pulling a dead man's coat flap over his face for warmth. Federal stretcher-bearers came and went, carrying off as many of the wounded as they could. Scavengers from both sides

Beneath a hill held by Stonewall Jackson's artillery, Federal burial parties inter the dead, many of whose uniforms and shoes have been removed during the night by Confederate scavengers. A Virginia soldier wrote in his diary that "all the Yank dead had been stripped of every rag of their clothing and looked like hogs that had been cleaned. It was an awful sight."

Saluted by both sides as "the angel of Marye's Heights," 19-year-old Sergeant Richard Kirkland of Company E, 2nd South Carolina Volunteers, repeatedly risked Federal fire on the day after the battle to carry water to parched, wounded Union soldiers still lying before the stone wall. A year later, Kirkland himself fell mortally wounded at Chickamauga.

roamed the battlefield, stripping the dead of their uniforms. "More than once," Colonel Chamberlain remembered, "I was startled from my unrest by someone turning back the coatskirt from my face, peering, half vampire-like, to discover if it too were of the silent and unresisting; turning away more disconcerted at my living word than if a voice had spoken from the dead."

After midnight, two brigades of Sykes's Federals were ordered to a forward position on the field. Captain John W. Ames of the 11th U.S. Infantry remembered a macabre scene as the men marched across the blasted plain: "Here stood a low brick house, with an open door in its gable end, from which shone a light, and into which we peered when passing. Inside sat a woman, gaunt and hard-featured, with crazy hair, still sitting by a smoking candle, though it was nearly two hours past midnight. But what woman could sleep, though ever so masculine and tough of fiber, alone in a house between two hostile armies — two corpses lying across her doorsteps, and within, almost at her feet, four more! So, with wild eyes and face lighted by her smoky candle, she stared across the dead barrier into the darkness outside with the look of one who heard and saw not, and to whom all sounds were a terror."

During the night, nature put on an unearthly show, as if to emphasize the awful events of the day just past. The sky was emblazoned with the fiery glow of the northern lights, seldom seen so far south. Some Confederates wondered whether a Federal supply depot had been put to the torch, while others decided, as one of them later phrased it, "that the heavens were hanging out banners and streamers and setting off fireworks in honor of our victory."

General Burnside spent most of the night visiting various units and conferring with their commanders, belatedly assessing the situation and agonizing over what to do next. He maintained a cheerful front, but as General Couch said later, "It was plain that he felt he had led us to a great disaster, and one knowing him so long and well as myself could see he wished his body was also lying in front of Marye's Heights. I never felt so badly for a man in my life."

In the early-morning hours, Burnside returned to his headquarters and ordered IX Corps to prepare to resume the attack when daylight came; apparently the distraught army commander intended to lead the advance in person. But around dawn on December 14, just before the new attack was to begin, General Sumner came to Burnside and objected vigorously to the plan. Burnside once again consulted his top commanders. Their advice was unanimous, and Burnside relented; there would be no further attacks.

At noon, General Burnside held another council of war. It was decided to withdraw

The Phillips House, near Falmouth, used by Burnside as his headquarters during and after the battle, accidentally caught fire and burned to a shell in February 1863. "Not a bucket of water could be had to quench the fire," lamented Burnside's provost marshal. "Wells all dry."

Franklin's troops on the south flank and Sumner's and Hooker's on the north. But the town would be held so that there would be something to show for the enormous sacrifice. All but 12,000 men would recross the river; Couch's II Corps and Butterfield's V Corps would be responsible for the continuing defense of Fredericksburg.

Meanwhile, all through the 14th the men on the field waited under fire for orders to move. "We laid up a breastwork of dead bodies," Colonel Chamberlain wrote. "We lay there all the long day, hearing the dismal thud of bullets into the dead flesh of our lifesaving bulwarks. No relief could dare to reach us."

Confederates behind the stone wall could hear the wounded men groaning and calling for water. After a time the appeals became more than Sergeant Richard Kirkland of the 2nd South Carolina could bear. The sergeant sought out General Kershaw and won his reluctant approval to take some water to the Federals on the field. Kershaw warned him that he might be shot, yet refused him permission to display a white handkerchief lest the Federals think that a parley was being requested. Kirkland went anyway, and spent hours tending to the men lying in misery on the cold, muddy ground. His name was remembered, and after the War a street in Fredericksburg was named in his honor.

By the night of December 15, the Federals had managed to withdraw their men from the battlefield. Under the cover of a driving rainstorm, the dispirited troops of the Army of the Potomac began their evacuation of Fredericksburg, crossing the Rappahannock on pontoon bridges that had been covered with dirt and straw to muffle the sound of tramping feet.

During the early-morning hours, Burnside had another change of heart. It was too dangerous, he decided, to try to defend the town with so small a force; the corps of Couch and Butterfield must leave as well. At 7:30 a.m. the last units — the 5th New York Zouaves and the Regulars of Sykes's division — crossed the river, and the pontoons were cut loose and taken up.

Ironically, the withdrawal proved to be the best-executed movement of the entire operation. The men of General Lee's command awoke on the morning of the 16th expecting that the Federals would resume their disastrous attacks — only to find that the entire army was gone.

A short time later the troops of Couch's II Corps, in camp near Falmouth, formed up for a review by General Burnside. Senior officers rode up and down the ranks, waving their caps and swords, trying to get the men to cheer the army commander. But all they could elicit were a few derisive catcalls.

"Give Us Victories"

"The army has become greatly disorganized. Our troops are rushed about, managed and maneuvered little better than a mob, and discipline is sinking to its lowest ebb. There is want of unity, accord and confidence in each other, in the general officers, and in the Administration. The remedy must begin at Washington."

BRIGADIER GENERAL GOUVERNEUR K. WARREN, V CORPS, ARMY OF THE POTOMAC

The news from Fredericksburg was greeted with jubilation throughout the South. The Richmond *Examiner* proclaimed a "stunning defeat to the invader, a splendid victory to the defender of the sacred soil." The Charleston *Mercury* exulted that "General Lee knows his business and the army has yet known no such word as fail." A correspondent for the *Mercury* reported from Virginia that the Confederate commander had cast aside his normal reserve, and was "jubilant, almost off balance, and seemingly desirous of embracing everyone who calls on him."

President Jefferson Davis was not immediately available to celebrate the triumph; he had left Richmond on December 10 for an extended journey through the Deep South and the Western theater of operations. But he returned to the Confederate capital on January 5, and a crowd gathered that evening at his residence to welcome him home.

The Chief Executive used the occasion to salute his army commander: "Our glorious Lee, the valued son, emulating the virtue of the heroic Light Horse Harry, his father, has achieved a victory at Fredericksburg, and driven the enemy back from his last and greatest effort to get on to Richmond." Davis conceded wryly that a few enemy soldiers had managed to reach Richmond — those taken prisoner at Fredericksburg. His quip drew appreciative laughter from the crowd.

There was, of course, no laughter in the North. As the wounded streamed back to Washington and long lists of the dead appeared in the newspapers, a mood of despondency settled over the Union, and cries for a negotiated peace were heard. Burnside and his subordinates were bitterly criticized for the defeat. As the Cincinnati *Commercial* exclaimed, "It can hardly be in human nature for men to show more valor or generals to manifest less judgment, than were perceptible on our side that day."

The main target of the attacks, however, was President Lincoln. Among his critics was the publisher of the influential Chicago *Tribune*, Joseph Medill, who laid the "central imbecility" of the Fredericksburg Campaign directly on the President. The respected historian and former U.S. Secretary of War, George Bancroft, castigated Lincoln and his associates. The President, he said, is "ignorant, self-willed, and is surrounded by men some of whom are as ignorant as himself." The Radical Republican Senator from Michigan, Zachariah Chandler, gloomily concluded that "the President is a weak man, too weak for the occasion, and those fool or traitor generals are wasting time and yet more precious blood in indecisive battles and delays."

Lincoln himself was distraught. Shortly after the battle, Governor Andrew Curtin of Pennsylvania paid a call at the White House. Curtin was fresh from a visit to the battlefield, and he painted a ghastly picture. "Mr. President," he said, "it was not

COLUMBIA. "Where are my 15,000 Sons—murdered at Fredericksburg?"   LINCOLN. "This reminds me of a little Joke—"   COLUMBIA. "Go tell your Joke AT SPRINGFIELD!!"

Reflecting the grief and rage felt in the North after Burnside's failure at Fredericksburg, a cartoon published in January 1863 shows the national symbol Columbia denouncing President Lincoln along with General in Chief Henry Halleck and Secretary of War Edwin Stanton. The caption makes a snide reference to Lincoln's well-known penchant for humorous anecdotes, and suggests he resign the presidency and return home to tell his jokes in Springfield, Illinois.

a battle, it was a butchery." Curtin reported that the President was "heart-broken at the recital, and soon reached a state of nervous excitement bordering on insanity." Lincoln described his own state of mind more succinctly: "If there is a worse place than hell, I am in it."

Burnside sent a report on the battle to General in Chief Halleck on December 17. In it, Burnside attributed the failure of his plan to the late arrival of the pontoons. But he manfully accepted full blame for the disaster: "The fact that I decided to move from Warrenton onto this line rather against the opinion of the President, Secretary and yourself, and that you have left the whole management in my hands, without giving me orders, makes me the more responsible."

After reading the official report the President, despite his anguish, framed a consoling reply — addressed not to Burnside, but to the Army of the Potomac. "Although you were not successful, the attempt was not an error, nor the failure other than accident," he wrote to the men. "The courage with which you, in an open field, maintained the contest against an entrenched foe, and the consummate skill and success with which you crossed and recrossed the river in the face of the enemy, show that you possess all the qualities of a great army, which will yet give victory to the cause of the country and of popular government. Condoling with the mourners for the dead, and sympathizing with the severely wounded, I congratulate you that the number is comparatively so small. I tender to you, officers and soldiers, the thanks of the nation."

Burnside remained determined to renew the offensive in the Fredericksburg area. He resolved to move his army a short distance up the Rappahannock, then cross and circle to the south to get behind Lee. Cavalry units would go first, crossing at Kelly's Ford, 25 miles northwest of the town, and severing the vital enemy supply routes on two railroads: the Virginia Central, and the Richmond, Fredericksburg & Potomac. On December 26, Burnside ordered supplies laid in for a 10-day movement and had the men cook three days' rations; all units were to be ready to march on 12 hours' notice.

The cavalry moved out on December 30 and had reached Kelly's Ford when Burnside received a cryptic telegram from the President: "I have good reason for saying that you must not make a general movement of the army without letting me know." The order came as a shock to Burnside, who thought his plans were known only to him and his staff. Mystified, he countermanded his orders and headed for Washington to find out what was going on.

Lincoln's message was the result of an intrigue by two of Burnside's officers, Brigadier Generals John Newton and John Cochrane of Franklin's grand division. Late in December, they had traveled to Washington to complain about Burnside to their Congressmen. But the two generals, neither of whom had a reputation for brilliance, had overlooked the fact that Congress adjourns for the holidays: Most of the Representatives were back in their home districts. Cochrane was a former congressman, which made the blunder all the more remarkable, but he compensated for it by arranging an appointment with Secretary of State William Seward. Seward in turn arranged for the generals to see the President.

The two officers hemmed and hawed in the presence of Lincoln, then finally got around to telling him of Burnside's planned attack. They predicted failure and expressed their concern that another defeat might well destroy the Army of the Potomac. On the strength of their reservations, Lincoln sent his curt telegram restraining Burnside.

The Army commander arrived at the White House on New Year's Day. When the President had explained the gist of the complaints without naming the two generals, Burnside demanded that the officers be dismissed from the service — whoever they were. Then Burnside unburdened himself of a greater worry. The disagreement between him and his subordinates over the projected operation was so deep, he said, that he was "not sustained in this by a single Grand Division commander." Moreover, since he had lost their confidence, perhaps he "ought to retire to private life." Burnside apparently went on to hint that he should not be the only one to go. Secretary of War Stanton and General in Chief Halleck also lacked the confidence of the army and the country, and Lincoln should think about replacing them.

The President was not prepared for all this, and he asked Burnside for time to think. Burnside went back to his headquarters, and Lincoln turned to Halleck for advice as to the army's next move. He wrote the general in chief a letter, asking him to go down to Fredericksburg and evaluate Burnside's new plan firsthand.

Lincoln was aware that Halleck rarely came down squarely on one side of an issue when he could avoid taking a stand. The President therefore accompanied his request with a blunt admonition: "If in such a difficulty as this you do not help, you fail me precisely in the point for which I sought your assistance. Your military skill is useless to me if you will not do this."

Halleck was offended and immediately threatened to resign. The beleaguered President officially withdrew the offending letter, and the ruffled general in chief stayed on the job. But he would not go to Fredericksburg.

Nor would he take a stand beyond agreeing with Burnside that the army ought to make some kind of move against the Confederates before it went into winter quarters. "As you yourself admit," Halleck wrote Burnside, once again passing the buck, "it devolves on you to decide upon the time, place and character of the crossing which you may attempt."

Lincoln added to Halleck's letter a less-than-ringing endorsement of Burnside and his plans. "I deplore the want of concurrence with you in opinion by your general officers, but I do not see the remedy. Be cautious, and do not understand that the Government or country is driving you. I do not yet see how I could profit by changing the command of the Army of the Potomac, and if I did, I should not wish to do it by accepting the resignation of your commission."

Burnside could not have found much comfort in his superiors' instructions to do something, but to be cautious; or in the assurance that he was not to be relieved. But he resolved nevertheless to implement his delayed plan to march a few miles upstream, cross the Rappahannock and outflank Lee. He admitted frankly to Lincoln, "I have no other plan of campaign for this winter."

Burnside's idea was sound, and it might have worked had the attack been launched a few weeks earlier, as he had intended. But in Virginia in January, military movements were thrall to a factor that not even Napoleon himself could control: the winter weather.

On January 20, Burnside proclaimed to his troops: "The auspicious moment seems to have arrived to strike a great and mortal blow to the rebellion, and to gain that decisive victory which is due to the country." Then he formed the Army of the Potomac into columns and, as a band played "Yankee Doodle," sent the men off. The skies were cloudy that morning, but the air was filled with optimism.

However, by dusk fog had moved in; by dark rain had begun to fall. The rain came down harder as the night progressed, and the wind rose. The men pitched their tents, and tried to start fires with tree branches that were too wet to burn. "It was a dismal night," recalled Colonel Regis de Trobriand of the 38th New York Infantry, "one of those sleepless nights when everything has funereal aspect, in which the enthusiasm is extinguished; in which courage is worn out, the will enfeebled and the mind stupefied."

By morning, the rain was falling in torrents. The roads were dissolving into ribbons of mud. The pontoon and artillery trains became backed up in a two-mile-long tangle, delaying the crossing of the Rappahannock all day. Wagons sank in up to their wheel hubs, and artillery pieces became mired so deeply that neither 12-horse teams nor gangs of 150 men hauling on ropes could pull them out. One team of mules sank deeper and deeper as it struggled to extricate a wagon; when the men hooked a chain around the neck of the leading mule and tried to free it, they broke the animal's neck. Dozens of horses and mules died of exhaustion. Others gave up the struggle and had to be killed. The men slipped, floundered and fell sprawling, their shoes sucked off by the mud. As Burnside rode along the column, an irreverent teamster whose mules were hopelessly mired doffed his cap and said, "General, the auspicious moment has arrived."

"Three times we started out," Private Alfred Davenport of the 5th New York wrote in a letter home, "but the roads were so blocked up we only made 1½ miles. Across the river the Rebels set up a big sign-board: 'Burnside's Army Stuck in the Mud,' and they were asking our pickets if they wanted any help laying pontoons, and so the Rebels seem to know everything we are doing anyway and laughing at us."

The rain continued without letup for nearly four days. By the time the storm abated, the army and its animals were worn out, and there was nothing to do but call off the movement and return to camp. Another offensive — soon to be labeled the "mud march" — had ended in ignominious failure.

Predictably, Burnside's officers condemned their commander for the fiasco.

General Hooker outdid them all, telling a newspaper correspondent that Burnside was incompetent and the Administration feeble. The country needed a dictator, Hooker said, and the sooner the better.

Burnside felt, with some justification, that his subordinates had betrayed him, and Hooker's outburst was more than he could stand. On January 23, the enraged commander wrote out General Order No. 8, one of the most remarkable and intemperate documents in the annals of the U.S. Army.

Burnside opened with a bitter indictment of Hooker. In nonstop legalistic language, Burnside charged the general with "unjust and unnecessary criticisms of the actions of his superior officers, and of the authorities, and having, by the general tone of his conversation, endeavored to create distrust in the minds of officers who have associated with him, and having, by omissions and otherwise, made reports and statements which were calculated to create incorrect impressions, and for habitually speaking in disparaging terms of other officers."

Burnside recommended that Hooker be dismissed from the service, "as a man unfit to hold an important commission during a crisis like the present, when so much patience, charity, confidence, consideration and patriotism are due from every soldier in the field." Moreover, Burnside wrote, Generals Franklin and Smith, and various other officers critical of his leadership — in particular Newton and Cochrane, whom Burnside had by this time identified as the generals who had gone to the President — should be relieved, or dismissed from the service.

Of course, Burnside did not have the authority to dismiss anyone from the Army without a court-martial — only the President

Late in January 1863, Federal infantrymen slog knee-deep across a rain-swollen stream during the infamous "mud march" — an attempted Union advance defeated by torrential downpours. A veteran wrote: "The bottom literally dropped out of the whole immediate country." The men, he added, were "wallowing, sliding and slipping at every step."

Officers of General Hooker's staff stage mock combat with sabers, bottles and shovels. Hooker tolerated such high jinks, which helped give his headquarters an unsavory reputation. It was "a combination barroom and brothel," sniffed one strait-laced officer from Boston.

Major General Joseph Hooker had a reputation for being fond of the bottle. Hooker claimed that he gave up drinking when he assumed command of the Army of the Potomac, but his troops persisted in singing a ditty that went in part, "Joe Hooker is our leader — He takes his whiskey strong!"

did. An aide to Burnside suggested that Lincoln should see the inflammatory document before it was published. The incensed general hurried to Washington and gave Lincoln both the order and his resignation; the President, he said, must accept one or the other.

Lincoln concluded that the situation could not be saved, and regretfully prepared orders relieving Burnside of his command. But the President insisted that Burnside's services were needed elsewhere and refused to accept his resignation from the Army. Burnside yielded, and later assumed command of the Department of the Ohio.

The order relieving Burnside also reassigned all three of his grand division commanders. Franklin was relieved and later given a minor command in Louisiana. Sumner, although he had not criticized Burnside, was relieved at his own request and ordered

to duty in Missouri; the stalwart old soldier went north for a rest before assuming his new command, took sick and died in Syracuse. The last general mentioned in the order was the obstreperous Joseph Hooker; to him went command of the Army of the Potomac.

The choice was a surprising one, in view of Hooker's intemperate remarks about his predecessor and about the need for a dictator at the country's helm. But Lincoln had to name someone, and he knew that among the various candidates Hooker had one compelling asset — a reputation in the discouraged, defeat-weary Union as a fighting general.

A West Point graduate, Hooker had served in the Mexican War, during which he had been brevetted for gallantry three times. Yet in the same conflict he had earned the undying enmity of General in Chief Winfield Scott for conspiring to have him removed,

and had become known for hard drinking and high living. Like many of his colleagues, Hooker left the Army after the Mexican War, and later failed miserably as a farmer in California. When the Civil War threatened, Hooker joined the California militia, then commanded by Henry Halleck, and rose to the rank of colonel.

When war came, Hooker resigned from the militia and headed for Washington. For a time he could not get a U.S. Army commission because General Scott remembered his insubordinate ways in the Mexican War. After watching the Federal debacle at the first Battle of Bull Run, the brash young civilian called on Lincoln at the White House and blurted out to the President with characteristic immodesty, "It is no vanity in me to say that I am a damned sight better general than any you, sir, had on that field."

The President decided to give him an opportunity to prove his contention, and Hooker was commissioned a brigadier general of volunteers. He earned a reputation as an aggressive commander in the campaign on the Peninsula, at Second Bull Run and at Antietam, and came to be known as "Fighting Joe" — at least partly because of a typographical error.

During the Peninsular Campaign, a typesetter for a New York newspaper labeled a story about the action around Williamsburg: "Fighting — Joe Hooker." The tag was only to identify the story at the newspaper and was not for publication; it meant simply that fighting was going on and that Hooker was involved in it. But the title was printed, inadvertently and without the dash, appearing as "Fighting Joe Hooker." The sobriquet stuck for the rest of his life. Hooker hated it. "Don't call me 'Fighting Joe,' " he once

Corps Badges for Instant Identification

One of General Hooker's most effective innovations in the spring of 1863 was an order that designated distinctive badges for each of his divisions and corps. The badges, worn by every soldier on his cap, would enable officers to tell at a glance in the heat of battle what unit any man belonged to; stragglers and deserters could be identified immediately by unit and sent back to the proper command.

As it happened, the badges helped boost morale. The men were proud of their outfits and viewed the emblems as marks of distinction.

The badges were simple geometric shapes cut from colored cloth. The shape denoted the corps, the color the division. So popular did they become that officers bought ornate versions in velvet and tinsel, while enlisted men fashioned variations from bone or even flattened bullets. Jewelers such as Tiffany in New York made versions in gold, silver and enamel, often engraved with the owner's name, unit and battle honors.

Before the War ended, the corps badges were made regulation throughout the U.S. Army.

A black felt hat, belonging to Lieutenant Henry Brewster of the 57th New York, bears the badge of the 1st Division, II Corps.

	1ST DIVISION	2ND DIVISION	3RD DIVISION
I CORPS			
II CORPS			
III CORPS			
V CORPS			
VI CORPS			
XI CORPS			
XII CORPS			

Gold and enamel I Corps badge, engraved with owner's unit and initials

Silver VI Corps pin, with red cross denoting the 1st Division

Trefoil II Corps badge of a member of the 34th New York

Bone V Corps badge made by Private John Hays, 5th New York

said, "for that name has done and is doing me incalculable injury. It makes a portion of the public think that I am a hot-headed, furious young fellow, accustomed to making furious and needless dashes at the enemy."

Still, Lincoln knew that Hooker could be arrogant and impulsive; he wanted to impress on the general that he would be expected to overcome such shortcomings, and fulfill the promise of his better qualities. On January 26, 1863, the President offered some stern advice in a remarkable letter to the new army commander.

"General," Lincoln wrote, "I have placed you at the head of the Army of the Potomac. Of course I have done this upon what appears to me to be sufficient reasons, and yet I think it best for you to know that there are some things in regard to which I am not quite satisfied with you. I believe you to be a brave and a skilful soldier, which, of course, I like. I also believe you do not mix politics with your profession, in which you are right. You have confidence in yourself, which is a valuable, if not an indispensable quality. You are ambitious, which, within reasonable bounds, does good rather than harm. But I think that during General Burnside's command of the army, you have taken counsel of your ambition, and thwarted him as much as you could, in which you did a great wrong to the country, and to a most meritorious and honorable brother officer.

"I have heard, in such a way as to believe it, of your recently saying that both the army and the government needed a dictator. Of course, it was not *for* this, but in spite of it, that I have given you the command. Only those generals who gain successes can set up dictators. What I now ask of you is military success, and I will risk the dictatorship. The

government will support you to the utmost of its ability, which is neither more nor less than it has done and will do for all commanders. I much fear that the spirit which you have aided to infuse into the army, of criticizing their commander, and withholding confidences from him, will now turn upon you. I shall assist you as far as I can to put it down. Neither you, nor Napoleon, if he were alive again, could get any good out of an army, while such a spirit prevails in it.

"And now, beware of rashness. Beware of rashness, but with energy and sleepless vigilance, go forward, and give us victories.

"Yours very truly, A. Lincoln."

Hooker carried the letter around in his pocket and read it to his friends. "He talks to me like a father," he said of the President. "I shall not answer this letter until I have won him a great victory."

Hooker's first task was to restore the army to fighting trim. The men had not tasted victory since Antietam in September, they had not been paid in six months, and they were falling sick by the thousands. Moreover, men were running away at an alarming rate. Those who remained in camp were either dejected or diseased, or both.

The army's medical inspector general, Thomas F. Perley, had said early in January: "I do not believe I have ever seen greater misery from sickness than now exists in our Army of the Potomac." Scurvy, dysentery and malnutrition were rife; Perley complained angrily about the shortage of proper food, especially fresh vegetables and bread.

Poor sanitation was also a factor. In the hills near Falmouth, the men had built a city of log and canvas huts in which they lived four to a shelter. Although the structures provided better protection from the winter weather than did tents, there were virtually no provisions for keeping the huts — or the men that lived in them — clean; disease was the inevitable result.

Hooker set about improving the lot of his troops with energy and determination. By enforcing sanitation regulations — requiring the use of proper latrines, regular bathing and frequent airing of bedding — and by improving rations, he quickly cut the sick call in half. Fresh bread, onions and potatoes were made available several times a week,

along with occasional rations of tobacco.

At the same time, Hooker initiated measures designed to discourage desertion. He granted regular furloughs and filled the empty hours of camp life with drills and instruction periods. The Congress, in the meantime, finally made arrangements to get the soldiers their back pay.

Hooker also revised his command structure. He scrapped Burnside's grand division arrangement and ordered his seven infantry corps commanders to report directly to him. He detached the cavalry units from the in-

An Inspirational "Grand Review"

In this sketch by a newspaper artist, General Hooker and a bareheaded, careworn President Lincoln review the cavalry. The troopers salute with dipped guidons and raised sabers.

During President Lincoln's visit to the Army of the Potomac in early April of 1863, General Hooker staged what one Pennsylvania officer termed "the most magnificent military pageant ever witnessed on this continent." Every soldier not on picket duty turned out for the President; first Lincoln rode by 15,000 cavalrymen (left), and then two days later, in what was ever after called the Grand Review, 85,000 infantrymen marched past in massed formations two companies wide (right).

Hooker held the review on a huge cleared field on Falmouth Heights, in full view of the Confederates at Fredericksburg. He wanted to impress them with the size and power of his Union force, and in that he succeeded.

As Hooker also intended, the review provided a tremendous morale boost for the Federal soldiers. The great parade burned in the memories of the men who took part. A New Yorker wrote home: "It was full of bright visions" as "brigade after brigade swept by in endless procession." An officer echoed: "I can still see that soul-thrilling column. How glad I am to have looked upon it."

A column of regiments, battle-torn flags flying, marches past the President at the double-quick during the Grand Review on April 8, 1863.

fantry divisions and organized a separate cavalry corps under Major General George Stoneman. Henceforth, Federal horsemen would operate as an autonomous force, carrying out large-scale screening, reconnaissance and offensive missions in the manner of Confederate General Jeb Stuart's celebrated legions. Hooker set up a Bureau of Military Information to compile and coordinate intelligence reports from such varied sources as cavalry patrols, a new corps of scouts, balloon observations, prisoners of war and enemy deserters.

The Army of the Potomac responded favorably to Hooker's efforts. Private Alfred Davenport of the 5th New York had written just after the change of command: "The men put no trust in Hooker's bluster, he will simply get us killed as Burnside did." But by March 27, Davenport's attitude had changed: "General Hooker has now a fine army in discipline, if not in numbers, and he has overhauled all the departments and made many useful and efficient changes. Our camps were never so clean and the food better, the introduction of soft bread was a

Regiments of Confederates relieve the tedium of their winter bivouac near Fredericksburg with a huge snowball fight that ultimately involved 9,000 officers and men. The good-humored battle was touched off on January 29, 1863, by spirited Texas and Georgia troops, many of whom had never seen snow before.

beneficial and humane act and he has our thanks for that, if nothing else. He is energetic, crafty and a fighting general."

On the other side of the river, winter brought far greater suffering to the Army of Northern Virginia. In January the Confederate command, chronically short of supplies, was forced to impose a further, drastic reduction in meat and sugar rations. By March, Lee lamented that there did not seem to be enough food to sustain the health and stamina of the men. "Symptoms of scurvy are appearing among them," he said, "and, to supply the place of vegetables, each regiment is directed to send a daily detail to gather sassafrass buds, wild onions, lamb's quarter, and poke sprouts; but for so large an army the supply obtained is very small."

Another desperate shortage, that of shoes and proper winter clothing, was outlined by a Louisiana staff officer in a letter to his Representative in the Confederate Congress. Of the 1,500 men available for duty in his brigade, the officer reported, 400 had no shoes. "These men, of course, can render no effective service," he said, "as it is impossible for them to keep up with the column in a march over frozen ground." Large numbers of men had no blankets, he reported, and some were without underclothing, shirts or socks. "Overcoats, from their rarity," he wrote, "are objects of curiosity."

The Confederates were also handicapped by an acute shortage of manpower. Lee's army, already heavily outnumbered at the Battle of Fredericksburg, was further depleted in February when Longstreet was dispatched with Pickett's and Hood's divisions to southern Virginia and coastal North Carolina to forage for provisions and defend rail-

A Confederate sentry in Lee's army stands guard in the snow while his comrades try to stay warm around fires or huddled in tents during the winter of 1862-1863. The camp shown was near Richmond; Lee had spread his force in a long arc southward from Fredericksburg, enabling the hungry troops to forage more widely.

road communications. Thus Lee lost the services of 13,000 troops and three of his most seasoned and reliable commanders.

With both Hooker and Lee preoccupied by supply and organization problems, there was little contact between the two armies during the late winter months except for a few cavalry raids and skirmishes. The largest and most important of these occurred in the vicinity of Kelly's Ford.

The raid was initiated by Federal Brigadier General William Averell, a division commander in General Stoneman's cavalry corps. In the beginning of March, Averell went to Hooker for permission to take his horsemen up the Rappahannock, cross the river and drive off the Confederate cavalry units reported to be in the area.

It seemed to Averell to be a good opportunity to test the new independent cavalry organization, and perhaps in the process change Hooker's low opinion of troopers—scathingly expressed on one recent occasion when Hooker had asked, "Who ever saw a dead cavalryman?"

Averell had a further, more personal motive. The Confederate cavalry commander in the Kelly's Ford area—Brigadier General Fitzhugh Lee, a nephew of Robert E. Lee—had attended West Point at the same time as Averell, and a spirited rivalry existed between the former classmates. Fitz Lee, as he was known, sent Averell messages taunting him about the inferiority of Federal cavalry. In his latest missive, Lee had dared his old friend to come across the river and bring some coffee with him.

With Hooker's approval, Averell eagerly accepted the challenge and set out with six full regiments and portions of two others—3,000 cavalrymen in all—together with a

Veteran Fighters of Lee's Legions

The determined-looking men portrayed here were all veterans of Robert E. Lee's Army of Northern Virginia, present for duty as the mild spring weather of 1863 presaged renewed clashes. Lee's force, smaller, hungrier and less well equipped than Hooker's Army of the Potomac, was nonetheless formidable: His troops were tightly disciplined, swift on the march, savage in combat, confident, and devoted to their commanders. "There never were such men in an army before," Lee himself said that spring. "They will go anywhere and do anything if properly led."

PRIVATE JAMES THOMPSON
Company B, 51st Virginia

PRIVATE GEORGE G. AYOCK
Company B, 30th North Carolina

CAPTAIN CHARLES J. GREEN
Company A, 47th Virginia

PRIVATE THOMAS FONDREN MCKIE
Company A, 11th Mississippi

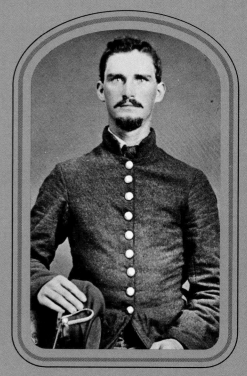

PRIVATE JOHN D. MILLER
Company H, 3rd South Carolina

CAPTAIN ASHER W. GARBER
Virginia Light Artillery

PRIVATE OTTO KEAN
Virginia Light Artillery

SERGEANT PAGE M. BAKER
1st Louisiana Special Battalion

PRIVATE THOMAS JEFFERSON GOLDMAN
Company D, 44th Georgia

PRIVATE SIMEON CHESTERFIELD PAYTES
Company C, 9th Virginia Cavalry

PRIVATE JOSEPH ABSALOM HIGGINBOTHAM
Company I, 19th Virginia

battery of artillery. The bulk of the horse-men arrived at Kelly's Ford on the morning of March 17.

First on the scene was an advance guard of the 4th New York Cavalry, commanded by Captain William Hart. The troopers soon spotted an abatis blocking the road on the far bank, and Hart sent a message back to Averell asking for men with axes to cut through the obstacle. Twenty dismounted troopers of the 16th Pennsylvania Cavalry soon arrived and waded into the frigid, waist-deep water, only to be driven back by heavy carbine fire from the Confederate defenders.

Two fieldpieces were then ordered forward to rake the Confederates; under the covering fire, Lieutenant Simeon Browne and 18 troopers of the 1st Rhode Island Cavalry rode into the ford, followed by the Pennsylvanians, who were still on foot and carrying their axes. Only three of the Rhode Island horsemen made it to the far shore, but these survivors and the Pennsylvanians gained a foothold and succeeded in breaching the abatis. More members of the 1st Rhode Island swiftly splashed across the stream, scattering the Confederate pickets and taking 25 prisoners.

When word of the encounter reached Fitz Lee at Culpeper, 10 miles west of the ford, he surmised that the Federals were moving against the Orange & Alexandria Railroad. He soon rode forward and deployed his 800 men — the 1st, 2nd, 3rd, 4th and 5th Virginia Cavalry Regiments — in a blocking position on the road between Kelly's Ford and Brandy Station, a small town on the railroad line six miles northwest of the ford.

As Fitz Lee's skirmishers probed forward toward the Rappahannock, they found to their surprise that the Federal cavalrymen,

some of them dismounted and stationed behind a stone wall, were deployed in defensive positions just a mile and a half from the ford. Averell, a conscientious and thorough professional soldier, was also a cautious one. He was not confident that his force outnumbered Fitz Lee's and had decided against rushing headlong into a fight with his resourceful classmate.

Averell faced some formidable opponents

William Averell, the 30-year-old brigadier general who led the Union cavalry in the clash at Kelly's Ford in March 1863, sits on a camp stool for a portrait with three of his officers in the summer of 1862. Only a fair student at West Point, Averell led his class in horsemanship, a skill that saw him through several brushes with death during the War.

Described as "a sturdy, muscular and lively little giant" by his rival William Averell, the bearded Confederate cavalryman Fitzhugh Lee sits for a photograph with Lieutenant Charles Minnegerode, a trusted aide.

he did not know about. By chance, Fitz Lee had at his side not only the redoubtable Jeb Stuart, but also the dashing artillery officer who had been the hero of Fredericksburg, Major John Pelham. Stuart had joined the action because he happened to be in Culpeper attending a court-martial. The handsome young Pelham, who was known for his interest in the ladies — "as grand a flirt as ever lived," said a friend — was there because he had wangled a brief leave of absence to pay a call on a young woman at nearby Orange Court House.

Fitz Lee ordered a squadron of the 3rd Virginia to dismount, take a forward position and open fire on the Federals behind the stone wall as a preliminary to a charge by the rest of the regiment; Stuart himself watched over the movement. Pelham went to the rear to advise Lee's artillery command-

er, Major James Breathed, in the placement of his guns, then dashed back to the front just as the mounted men of the 3rd Virginia reached the wall.

The troopers turned to their left, firing at the Federals with their pistols as they rode, searching for an opening or a low spot in the wall where they could break through. As they approached the Federal right, they were joined by troopers of the 5th Virginia. Pelham drew his sword, spurred his borrowed horse and galloped across the field at an angle to join the charge at its head.

Just as Pelham caught up with the Virginians, they found a gate and poured through it to try to turn the Federal right. Pelham reined in, stood in his stirrups, waved his sword and shouted "Forward!" to encourage the attacking horsemen. Just then a shell exploded with a flash and a roar above Pelham's head, knocking him from his horse to the ground. As he lay there, his eyes were open and there was no visible sign of a wound. But a sliver of metal had entered the back of his head, damaging vital nerves.

Two cavalrymen placed Pelham across a horse and took him to the rear. His heart was still beating and he survived an ambulance ride to Culpeper. There surgeons discovered the head wound. But before they could do anything to help him, he drew a deep breath and died.

Shortly after Pelham was hit, a Federal countercharge drove the 3rd and 5th Virginia from the stone wall. Meanwhile, on the Federal left, Averell's most dashing subordinate, Colonel Alfred Duffié, moved up his 1st Brigade, hoping to entice the rest of the Confederate cavalry into attacking his position. The 1st, 2nd and 4th Virginia obliged — and were startled to find Duffié responding with a charge of his own. As Duffié's four regiments swept forward, the outnumbered Confederates turned to retreat, but not in time for all of them to escape. A number of Virginians were killed or captured in the melee. One particularly intrepid Federal horseman, Lieutenant Nathaniel Bowditch of the 1st Massachusetts Cavalry, rushed ahead and slashed three grayclad horsemen from their mounts with his saber before he too fell, mortally wounded.

Duffié's success did not embolden Averell, however, and he ordered the charging horsemen to rein in. Then he mandated a cautious pursuit, halting once again barely a mile beyond the stone wall. Fitz Lee's horsemen charged this line, reinforcing Averell's conviction that he faced a strong enemy. At this point he learned from Confederate prisoners that Jeb Stuart was in the fight. This news quenched any desire Averell might have had for further action. As he later wrote, he "deemed it proper to withdraw."

A bugle sounded recall, and the Federal

Confederate artillerist Major John Pelham, killed at Kelly's Ford at the age of 25, was raised on an Alabama plantation, one of six sons of a physician. Pelham's bravery at Fredericksburg elicited a tribute from General Robert E. Lee: "It is glorious to see such courage in one so young."

At Kelly's Ford on March 17, the 1st Rhode Island and 6th Ohio ride headlong into the 4th Virginia (*far left*) in one of the War's first large-scale cavalry charges.

troopers headed back across the Rappahannock. Averell left behind two wounded Confederate officers, a sack of coffee and a message for his old classmate: "Dear Fitz. Here's your coffee. Here's your visit. How do you like it?"

The engagement was notable on two accounts. The Federal cavalry corps in its first large-scale fight had demonstrated unprecedented spirit. And the engagement had cost the Confederates dearly. They had lost 133 men, compared with the Federals' 78 casualties, and the price was magnified by the death of one of the Confederate Army's most promising young officers.

John Pelham was revered in the South, and he held a special place in the esteem of both his commander, General Stuart, and his general in chief, Robert E. Lee. Accompanied by a guard of honor, the body of the fallen artilleryman was taken to lie in state at the Capitol at Richmond, then was returned to Pelham's native Alabama. Said Stuart: "The gallant Pelham, so noble, so true, will be mourned by the nation."

As spring arrived and the Virginia roads dried out, the time approached for General Hooker's army to make its move. Hooker was supremely confident, or appeared so. With what he called "the finest army on the planet," he boasted to visitors that he could go all the way to New Orleans if he wanted to. "If the enemy does not run," he was heard to say, "God help them."

The army seemed to have caught his ebullient mood, and yet not everyone in the Federal camp was impressed. One of the visitors to headquarters was President Lincoln, who stayed in Falmouth for a few days in early April to take the measure of his new commander. As he listened to Hooker repeatedly use the phrase, "when I get to Richmond," the President must have flinched to hear yet another general intent on taking a city instead of destroying an enemy army. Moreover, Lincoln was always made uncomfortable by braggadocio, and on one occasion he interrupted Hooker to amend the pet phrase by saying, "*If* you get to Richmond, General." But the bumptious Hooker retorted, "Excuse me, Mr. President, but there is no *if* in this case. I am going straight to Richmond if I live."

Lincoln said later: "That is the most depressing thing about Hooker. It seems to me that he is overconfident." Then, pondering that aspect of the general's character, he offered an earthy analogy. "The hen is the wisest of all the animal creation," he said, "because she never cackles until after the egg is laid."

Before he left Falmouth, Lincoln sent for Hooker and General Darius Couch, now second in command of the army. The President distilled his parting advice into a single, prophetic sentence: "Gentlemen, in your next fight, *put in all your men.*"

Rebirth of a Beaten Army

THE 110th PENNSYLVANIA FORMED FOR INSPECTION

Bloodied and discouraged after the disaster at Fredericksburg, the Army of the Potomac went into winter quarters near the town of Falmouth, Virginia, across the Rappahannock from the scene of their December defeat. There a remarkable transformation took place. During the long lull in the fighting, the demoralized army, rife with desertions and disease, again became a powerful, confident force.

Much of the credit went to a new commander, Major General Joseph Hooker, who improved rations and medical care. But the men and their officers, with the timeless ingenuity of troops in the field, helped to ease their own lot. The soldiers neatly "logged up their tents," as the phrase went (*above, right*), making them tight against wind and snow. They also organized baseball games, boxing matches and, on St. Patrick's Day, an athletic meet that included a riotous horse race. By the time Hooker's forces broke camp in late April, a veteran recalled, "the discipline and morale of the army were about perfect." The troops, one soldier reported, "were once more ready to fight."

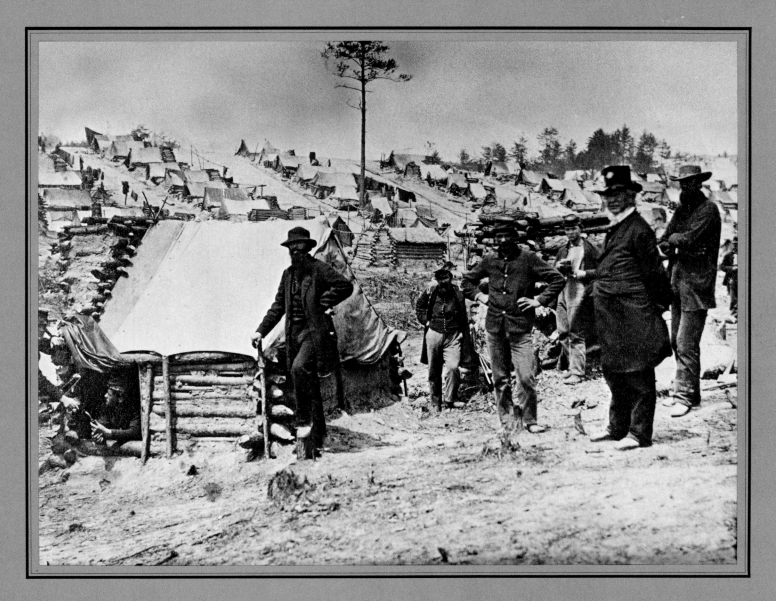

A ROTUND CHAPLAIN WITH PENNSYLVANIA MEN IN CAMP

A VISITING OFFICER'S WIFE ON A CAVALRY HORSE

GUARDS AT THE PROVOST MARSHAL'S OFFICE

LAUNDRY TIME IN THE PENNSYLVANIANS' CAMP

MEN OF THE 12TH NEW YORK AMID ABANDONED WINTER HUTS

CAPTAINS WILLIAM CANDLER, HARRY RUSSELL AND ALEXANDER MOORE OF GENERAL HOOKER'S STAFF

OFFICERS OF THE 1ST NEW YORK LIGHT ARTILLERY REGIMENT

The Panic on the Right

"Infantry, artillery, cavalry, panic-stricken cattle, accompanied with the shrieks of the wounded and groans of the dying, with a hail of shells from Jackson's guns and serenaded by the rebel yell, with officers cursing and everything in a chaotic state, was an experience I will never forget."

PRIVATE NATHANIEL BEERLY, 148TH PENNSYLVANIA, AT CHANCELLORSVILLE

As fine spring weather dried the roads, there was ever-increasing pressure on General Hooker to resume the offensive. Clearly, he would have to make his move during April. The President was now desperate for a victory to revive the Union's sagging morale. And with the Confederate forces at Fredericksburg depleted by the absence of Longstreet's two divisions, the Army of the Potomac enjoyed an enormous numerical superiority over the Army of Northern Virginia — roughly 135,000 to 60,000. But the advantage could not last. Longstreet might return at any time, and worse yet, 27,000 Federal troops whose enlistments would expire in May could not be counted on to reenlist.

A renewal of the attack at Fredericksburg was out of the question. In the months that had passed since the ghastly events of December 13, the Confederates had greatly improved their defenses there. Hooker felt sure that his army had been restored to effectiveness, but he dared not test the massed troops and bristling guns on Marye's Heights.

The Federals would have to flank the enemy position — not a simple task. On the left, downstream, the river widened steadily, and it was swollen by the spring runoff, making a successful crossing doubtful.

The prospects were not much more promising to Hooker's immediate right. Banks' Ford, five miles northwest of the town, and United States Ford, seven miles beyond that, were heavily guarded by the Confeder-

ates. But farther up, above the confluence of the Rapidan and Rappahannock Rivers, both streams could be crossed readily with little likelihood of serious resistance.

On April 11, Hooker informed President Lincoln that General George Stoneman would launch the campaign with 10,000 horsemen of his recently created cavalry corps. They were to cross the Rappahannock at least 20 miles upstream, then ford the Rapidan and get behind the Confederate army, severing its lines of communication.

Hooker persisted in the curious notion that Robert E. Lee and his army would be demoralized by the first show of force. "I am apprehensive that he will retire from before me the moment I should succeed in crossing the river," Hooker wrote the President, "and thus escape being seriously crippled." If that happened, Hooker hoped that the cavalry would "hold him and check his retreat until I can fall on his rear."

The loquacious Hooker was oddly reticent about exactly how the main body of his army would attack. He told his corps commanders nothing, and all he would say to the President was that, while the cavalrymen were moving, "I shall threaten the passage of the river at various points, and after they have passed well to the enemy's rear, shall endeavor to effect the crossing."

Stoneman set out on the morning of April 13. While most of his 10,000 troopers proceeded up the Rappahannock at a leisurely

118

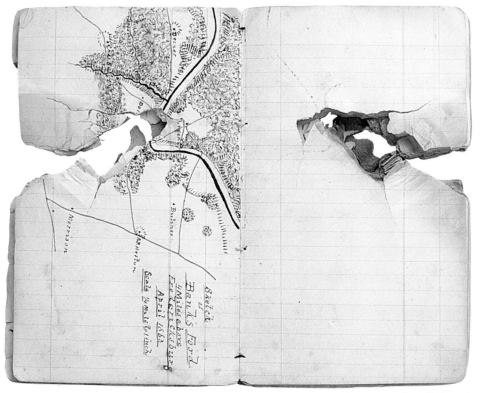

This torn notebook, open to a sketch of Banks' Ford on the Rappahannock River, was carried by Captain James Boswell, Stonewall Jackson's trusted 24-year-old chief engineer. The slender book failed to stop the bullet that killed Boswell at Chancellorsville; in the same volley that felled him, Jackson was mortally wounded.

cavalry, prevented now from crossing anywhere, set up camp a dozen miles north of the Rappahannock to await better weather.

On April 15, Hooker, certain his orders had been carried out, wrote Lincoln that, regardless of the storm, Stoneman's troopers had crossed the river. That evening, however, Hooker was forced to revise his optimistic report, informing the President that only one division had crossed. In fact, no Federal cavalrymen were south of the Rappahannock.

Despite the false reports, Lincoln sized up the situation at once; his ability to detect a fiasco in the making was by now finely tuned. Late on April 15 he wrote to Hooker: "General S. is not moving rapidly enough to make the expedition come to anything. He has now been out three days, two of which were unusually fair weather, and all three without hindrance from the enemy, and yet he is not 25 miles from where he started. I greatly fear it is another failure already."

It was. The rain continued to fall, and the river remained impassable for the better part of two weeks. Not only the cavalry, but the entire army, poised for movement and battle, was required to sit still in the mud. "The longer it rains the harder it seems to come down," Captain William Candler of Hooker's staff wrote on April 24. "Everyone is moving around in an aimless, nervous way, looking at the clouds and then at the ground, and in knots trying to convince themselves that it is going to clear off and they will be able to move day after tomorrow."

In fact, the weather did clear the next day, April 25. Brisk winds dried the mud and cloudless skies promised an end to the rainy spell. At this point, General Hooker decided to adopt a bold new strategy. The cavalry would go ahead with its mission to get be-

pace, he sent ahead a brigade under Colonel Benjamin "Grimes" Davis. Davis' men were to cross at Sulphur Springs, more than 30 miles northwest of Fredericksburg, and then double back down the Rappahannock to drive off the Confederate pickets at Freeman's and Beverly Fords. This would clear the way for the rest of the cavalry to cross.

Davis and his brigade successfully crossed the Rappahannock and beat back Confederate detachments guarding the fords. But the rest of Stoneman's troopers were slow to arrive — and then the skies opened on the hapless horsemen. As the rain fell, the Rappahannock rose alarmingly. Davis was forced to hasten back across the river to avoid having his small force trapped on the Confederate side. As it was, several men and horses were drowned while trying to negotiate the raging stream. Stoneman's main body of hind Lee and cut his supply lines. But instead of waiting for Stoneman's troopers to complete their mission, Hooker would simultaneously launch his infantry on a daring strategic envelopment. This campaign, unlike the recent brutal contest at Fredericksburg, would be a chess game for generals.

Hooker planned to move one third of his army — the V, XI and XII Corps — up the Rappahannock *(map, page 122)*, bypassing the heavily defended Banks' and United States Fords and crossing at Kelly's Ford, 20 miles upstream from Fredericksburg. Oliver Howard's XI Corps and Henry Slocum's XII Corps would head south and cross the Rapidan at Germanna Ford. George Meade's V Corps would double back toward Fredericksburg, crossing the Rapidan at Ely's Ford and driving the Confederates from the Banks' and United States Fords. This would open the way for Darius Couch's II Corps to cross the Rappahannock.

Couch was to await orders at the river, but the other three corps — Meade's, Slocum's and Howard's — were to reunite 10 miles west of Fredericksburg, at a rural crossroads marked by a large red-brick, white-columned mansion called Chancellor House. From it the country crossroads derived its presumptuous name — Chancellorsville.

To distract the Confederates from the threat to their left flank, Hooker planned a series of deceptions. General John Sedgwick would lead his own VI Corps and General John Reynolds' I Corps across the Rappahannock below Fredericksburg to feign a major attack on Stonewall Jackson's troops on the Confederate right. To confuse Robert E. Lee's scouts even further, two other Federal units — Daniel Sickles' III Corps and a II Corps division under John Gibbon —

would remain temporarily in their camps on Stafford Heights and at Falmouth, both clearly visible to Confederate pickets.

The Federal troops began their movement on the morning of April 27, with Stoneman's cavalry heading south on the next day. The three leading infantry corps found the Rappahannock at Kelly's Ford swollen by the recent rains, but crossed without delay on pontoon bridges laid by the engineers. By the morning of April 30, the three corps were across the Rapidan as well, and advancing to the southeast through the desolate expanse of scrub pine, oak and dense underbrush known as the Wilderness. By noon Meade's V Corps had arrived at the 50-acre clearing around Chancellorsville; by 2 p.m. Slocum had reached the Chancellor House at the head of XII Corps, with Howard's XI Corps following. Simultaneously, Couch's II

Corps, having been ordered forward, was preparing to cross the Rappahannock at United States Ford, which the Confederate pickets had abandoned when threatened from the rear.

Although the march was running six to nine hours behind schedule, Hooker's plan appeared to be working perfectly. "This is splendid, Slocum," exulted General Meade when the two generals met at the Chancellorsville crossroads, "we are on Lee's flank and he does not know it." Then, having not yet received word from Hooker but assuming that the Federal forces would press their advantage, Meade added, "You take the Plank Road toward Fredericksburg, and I'll take the Pike, or vice versa, as you prefer, and we will get out of this Wilderness."

Meade was startled by Slocum's response: "My orders are to take up a line of battle here, and not to move forward without further orders." Hooker, it turned out, was determined to wait for additional forces. Couch had not yet arrived. And Sickles' III Corps, summoned from Falmouth Heights, would not reach Chancellorsville until the next morning. Without these two corps, Hooker declined to move any closer to the Confederates.

Hooker seemed to believe that his successful flank march had already decided the contest. That evening he arrived in Chancellorsville and issued an order hailing the army's progress in triumphant terms: "The operations of the last three days have determined that the enemy must either ingloriously fly or come out from behind his entrenchments and give us battle on our own ground, where certain destruction awaits him."

At Fredericksburg, Robert E. Lee was growing increasingly nervous. "I feel by no means strong," he had written to President Jefferson Davis on April 27, "and from the condition of our horses and the amount of our supplies, I am unable even to act on the defensive as vigorously as circumstances may require." Lee was fully aware of the Federal army's numerical superiority. Worse, his scouts had been unable to divine where Hooker would strike next. Word came from Jeb Stuart on the 28th that "a large body of infantry and artillery was passing up the river," but there was no way of knowing whether this was a feint, an expedition to the Shenandoah Valley — or something else. The first sign of what Hooker might have in mind came the next day on the old battlefield south of Fredericksburg, near Hamilton's Crossing, where Jubal Early's division of Stonewall Jackson's corps was stationed.

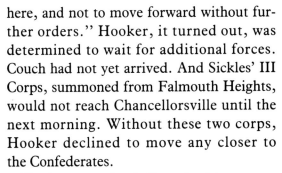

From winter camp north of the Rappahannock, the Army of the Potomac's V Corps embarks in late April on the march around Lee's flank — 56 miles in four days. "This march was a very trying one," wrote a member of the 5th New York Zouaves (*foreground*). "The roads were strewn with knapsacks and superfluous clothing accumulated during the winter months, which were thrown away by the men."

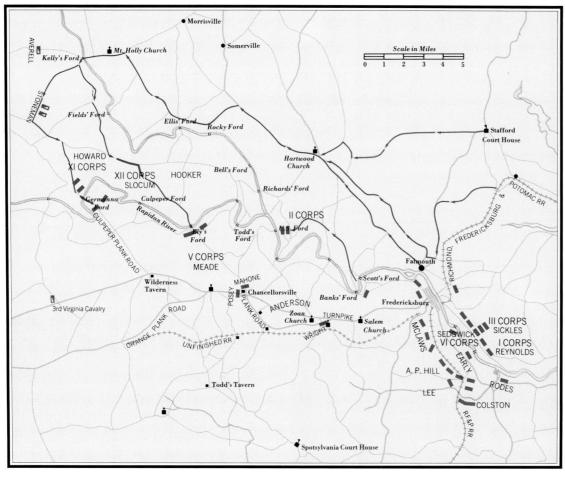

Hooker's bold flank march around Lee unfolds according to plan: While the Federal left wing under John Sedgwick demonstrated south of Fredericksburg, the corps of George Meade, Oliver Howard and Henry Slocum marched northwest and crossed the Rappahannock at Kelly's Ford on April 29. The three corps crossed the Rapidan at Germanna and Ely's Fords the next day to converge on Chancellorsville. Lee, still uncertain of Hooker's intention, sent Richard H. Anderson's division west to meet the Union threat to his left.

The enemy movement caught the celebrated Jackson during a rare interlude of relaxation. He had not been home in two years, had not seen his wife for nearly one year, and had never laid eyes on his only child. Taking advantage of the early-spring lull, he had brought his wife and infant daughter to his headquarters at the Yerby House, a mansion near Hamilton's Crossing.

They had spent eight days together when, on the morning of April 29, Jackson was awakened to hear that General Sedgwick was launching Hooker's long-awaited offensive; Federal troops were pouring over pontoon bridges thrown across the Rappahannock during the night. Jackson made preparations to send his wife and baby home, said a long good-by and rode to the front.

Jubal Early had already deployed his regiments on the plain near the Old Richmond Road and along the railway embankment when Jackson arrived, and Brigadier General Robert Rodes was in motion, marching up to reinforce Early. Sending an aide to alert Lee, Jackson ordered A. P. Hill to bring his division into line along the crest of the ridge to Early's right. Lee soon rode out to confer with Jackson, and then sent a request for reinforcements to President Davis.

As the day progressed, evidence of the

true Federal intentions began to accumulate. Sedgwick's troops at Hamilton's Crossing, although poised to attack, made no move. Then Lee received word that 14,000 men — General Howard's XI Corps — had crossed the Rappahannock at Kelly's Ford. Perhaps, Lee speculated, Howard was heading for the railroad junction at Gordonsville to harass Confederate supply lines. Toward evening, however, more information came from west of Fredericksburg. Couriers reported that Federal cavalry and infantry had crossed the Rapidan at Germanna and Ely's Fords. From those fords the roads converged on Chancellorsville. The threat to the Confederate left was growing, and Lee decided to send Major General Richard Anderson's division toward Chancellorsville to cover the roads leading to Fredericksburg.

Anderson moved out during the night of

In this torn sketch made at Falmouth Heights by a newspaper artist, aeronaut Thaddeus Lowe's observation balloon sits half-hidden in a grove of trees with its mobile hydrogen-gas generators nearby. In late April and early May, Lowe made several ascents over Fredericksburg, reporting to General Hooker that the Confederate line "appeared quite thin," and later that "nearly all of the enemy's units have been withdrawn" toward Chancellorsville. But his observations were not effectively used.

the 29th. Reaching the area of the Chancellor House, he confirmed that a large enemy force was bearing down from the west. He decided to withdraw from the tangled Wilderness, where maneuver was difficult, and take up a defensive position in open country. He selected a ridge near the Tabernacle Church and just west of a fork in the Plank Road that led from Fredericksburg. The two roads that ran westward from the fork — the Plank Road arcing to the south and a more northerly route known as the Turnpike — came back together at Chancellorsville. Thus Anderson's division covered both of the main routes the Federals might take.

At dawn on April 30, General Lee was still trying to decide what to do. As usual, he preferred to attack when in a tight situation. Yet he remained unsure of where he should strike. Jackson thought that Sedgwick offered an inviting target, but Lee, worried by the artillery still massed on the heights across the Rappahannock, did not agree.

By late afternoon, Sedgwick still had made no move to advance out of his bridgehead below Fredericksburg. His inaction, along with further reports of the Federal concentration at Chancellorsville, at last convinced Lee that the real threat lay to the west. Lee now gambled everything on his judgment, issuing orders for a general movement toward Chancellorsville. Jackson was instructed to leave only Early's division in front of Sedgwick's troops. The rest of Jackson's corps would march westward at dawn on May 1 to join Anderson near the Tabernacle Church. McLaws was to leave a brigade on the ridge beyond the town and follow with the rest of his division as swiftly as he could.

When Jackson reached his objective at 8 a.m. on the 1st, he found Anderson's men

busily digging in. With an army of superior numbers advancing toward them, it was just the thing to do. But it was not Jackson's way, under any circumstances, to wait for the enemy. He ordered Anderson's men to pack their tools and prepare to attack.

On the same morning, Hooker slowly advanced eastward out of Chancellorsville. Slocum's XII Corps and Howard's XI Corps moved out on the right, along the Plank Road, while just to the north Generals George Sykes and Winfield Scott Hancock

A lieutenant of the 1st New York Artillery inspects his battery of bronze 12-pounder Napoleons on the eve of the Battle of Chancellorsville. "The army prided itself upon its artillery, which was perhaps equal to any in the world," wrote Darius Couch, the Federal II Corps commander.

the Wilderness, the vanguard began to exchange fire with skirmishers from McLaws' division. Instead of recoiling before the Federal advance, Jackson ordered Anderson's men forward, and they began to assail the Federal division on both flanks. Sykes reported his situation, and Hooker ordered up Hancock's division. Hancock moved forward and occupied a ridge in open country. Slocum was also holding a strong position, off to the right, and Meade was advancing unmolested along the River Road.

Thus far the Federals had suffered little damage; they had responded quickly and gained strong positions on high ground, and were ready to move forward again. Yet suddenly, Hooker ordered his astonished corps commanders to break off the advance, abandon the ridges they held and return to the positions they had occupied the night before around Chancellorsville.

Hooker's subordinates could not believe their ears. "My God!" Meade exploded, "If we can't hold the top of a hill, we certainly cannot hold the bottom of it." Couch sent an aide to Hooker's headquarters to protest the order, but Hooker was adamant.

On their return to Chancellorsville, the troops were ordered to dig in. Couch, fuming, went to the army commander's headquarters, where Hooker tried to reassure him. "It is all right, Couch," Hooker said. "I have got Lee just where I want him; he must fight me on my own ground."

In the midst of a major offensive, at the first sting of enemy opposition, "Fighting Joe" Hooker had abandoned the attack and had gone over to the defensive. "To hear from his own lips," Couch wrote later, "that the advantages gained by the successful marches of his lieutenants were to culminate

marched their divisions along the Turnpike. Meade's V Corps advanced on the Federal left down the River Road, a rough trail between the Turnpike and the Rappahannock.

Everything seemed to be in Hooker's favor. He had 70,000 troops moving out smartly against 40,000 Confederates. Hooker said that God Almighty could not stop him from destroying the Rebel army, and while the remark offended some of the more devout members of his command, it appeared to be based on sound military judgment.

As Sykes's division reached the far edge of

in fighting a defensive battle in that nest of thickets was too much, and I retired from his presence with the belief that my commanding general was a whipped man."

The debate over what triggered Hooker's stunning loss of nerve began at once. A few blamed it on alcohol, but most who were around Hooker at the time disagreed. Several of his generals subsequently testified before the Committee on the Conduct of the War that Hooker was not drunk. General Couch, for one, said he believed that Hooker had "abstained from the use of ardent spirits" during the advance. Indeed, Couch and others suspected that a drink or two might have improved Hooker's performance.

Hooker himself later offered an explanation for his failure during the opening shots of the battle, and whiskey had nothing to do with it. "For once," he said simply, "I lost confidence in Hooker."

That evening, Generals Lee and Jackson met in the forest off the Plank Road south of Chancellorsville, near an ironworks called Catherine Furnace. There they reviewed the events of the day and made plans. Jackson was struck by Hooker's timidity and thought that the entire Federal army might withdraw across the river during the night.

Lee doubted it would be that easy. He believed that Hooker wanted the Confederates to attack him where he was, and Lee was inclined to oblige. The only question was where to strike. Lee ruled out an attack against the Federals' left flank, between the Rappahannock and the Turnpike, because of the dense trees and underbrush there. The generals sent two engineers out to reconnoiter the enemy center, around Chancellorsville.

Then Jeb Stuart rode up to Lee and Jackson with the news that Fitzhugh Lee's cavalry had scouted the Federal right. It was located about two miles to the northwest, along the road leading west from Chancellorsville, and was "in the air," meaning that it was not anchored on any natural terrain feature and was vulnerable. Soon the engineers returned to say that the combination of dense growth and abatis along the Federal center made the line there invulnerable. The Federal right must be turned, Lee said, and left Jackson to figure out a way to do it.

Before dawn, Jackson dispatched his topographical engineer, Major Jedediah Hotchkiss, to gather information about roads from the owner of Catherine Furnace, Colonel Charles Wellford. Before long, Hotchkiss returned with a detailed map he had sketched with Wellford's help.

Hotchkiss had learned of a concealed

This map of the opposing forces at Chancellorsville on May 2 traces Stonewall Jackson's furtive march parallel to the Federal front. Rear elements of Jackson's column were observed passing Catherine Furnace, and two divisions of Daniel Sickles' Federal III Corps attacked the column, taking several hundred prisoners. But the Confederate brigades of James Archer and Edward Thomas turned and threw back Sickles. Jackson, his intention still concealed, reached the Union army's exposed right flank with the bulk of his corps and attacked the unsuspecting Federal XI Corps.

Seated on hardtack boxes in the woods near Chancellorsville, Generals Lee (left) and Jackson quietly make plans to divide their forces and attack Hooker's Federals. Lee holds a map, drawn by Jackson's topographical officer, that charts the concealed route to Hooker's right flank.

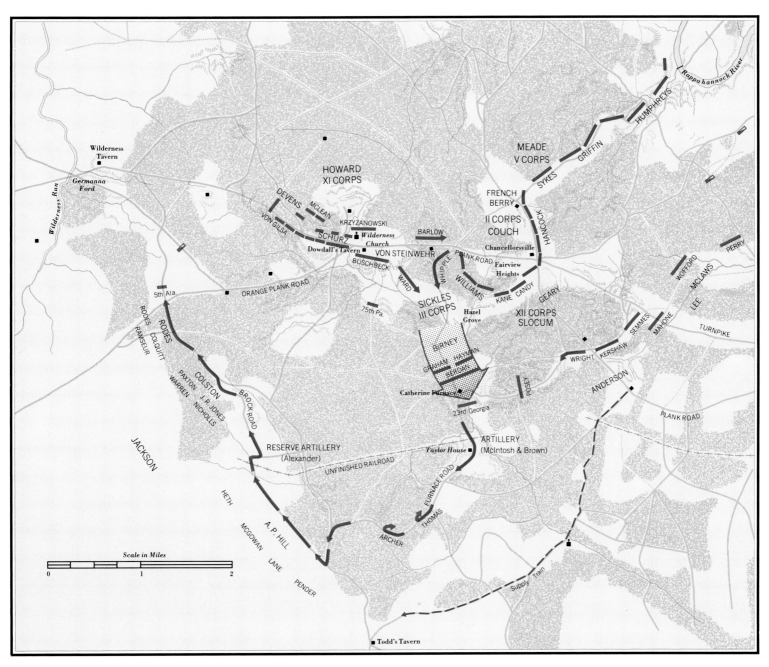

route of march to the Federal right flank. From Catherine Furnace a road ran southwest to the Brock Road. On the Brock Road the troops could move northwest, eventually gaining the Orange Plank Road, which would lead them back east toward Chancellorsville and the Federal lines.

The two generals listened intently, then engaged in a typically laconic exchange of enormous portent. "General Jackson, what do you propose to do?" Lee asked.

"Go around here," said Jackson, indicating the route on Hotchkiss' map.

"What do you propose to make this movement with?" Lee inquired.

"With my whole corps," said Jackson. Asked what troops he would leave behind to hold Hooker's army in check while the move was being made, Jackson said crisply, "The divisions of Anderson and McLaws."

Jackson was proposing one of the most daring gambles of the War. With the Army of Northern Virginia outnumbered by more than 2 to 1 overall, and already divided between Fredericksburg and Chancellorsville, he was suggesting a further division of forces in the face of the enemy. Leaving only 14,000 men with Lee to face Hooker's 75,000 head-on, Jackson would take 26,000 men through the woods to Hooker's right flank. His troops would have to march 12 miles; it would take all day, during which time they would be strung out along the roads and out of touch with Lee. Despite the danger, Lee's response was unhesitating. "Well," he said, "go on."

Shortly after 8 a.m. on May 2, Jackson's column came striding through the woods past a crossroads where Lee stood watching. Jackson, riding alongside his men, met the gaze of his commanding general and pointed in the direction of the flanking march. Lee nodded, and Jackson rode on.

The weather was warm that spring morning as the 10-mile-long column of infantrymen snaked through the woods. The men were in high spirits and moved along at a good pace, marching for 50 minutes and then resting for 10. Yet it was nothing like the clip that Jackson's so-called "foot cavalry" had maintained in the Valley Campaign a year before. The long hard winter had taken its toll, and soldiers who had been forced to subsist on little more than wild onions, sassafrass buds and poke sprouts had lost some of the snap from their stride.

Jackson rode in the vanguard, an oilcloth raincoat draped over his shoulders and his cap pulled down to his eyes. Leaning forward on his horse as if to speed the march, he continually urged the troops on. "Press forward!" he called. "See that the column is kept closed. Press on, press on!"

Hooker's line formed an arc that ran southwestward from the Rappahannock, curved around Chancellorsville and then jutted northwestward to its terminus along the Turnpike beyond the Wilderness Chapel. Meade's V Corps, anchored on the river about a mile downstream from United States Ford, held the left; the corps of Couch, Slocum and Sickles were deployed in the immediate area of the Chancellorsville crossroads; and Howard's XI Corps manned the right.

Brigadier General David Birney, a division commander in Sickles' corps, spotted Jackson's movement from his vantage point on a ridge known as Hazel Grove, roughly a mile southwest of Chancellorsville. As early as 8 a.m., Birney began dispatching couriers to tell General Hooker that a large Confederate force was moving from left to right across his front. For a time Hooker could see the column for himself as it came into view while crossing a hill.

Puzzled, Hooker spread out a map and studied the roads marked on it. "It can't be retreat," Hooker muttered to himself. "Retreat without a fight? That is not Lee. If not retreat, what is it?" he asked, and then answered his own question correctly: "Lee is trying to flank me."

Hooker dashed off a message to General Howard, whose troops were deployed to defend against an attack from the south; Hooker warned the XI Corps commander to be prepared for a flank attack from the west. "We have good reason to suppose that the enemy is moving to our right," Hooker explained. Howard was ordered to push his pickets well out to keep track of the enemy's movements.

Howard reported at 11 a.m.: "I am taking measures to resist an attack from the west." Because he did not check, Hooker did not know that all Howard had done was to face two regiments and his reserve artillery to the

Major General Daniel E. Sickles, commanding the Federal III Corps at Chancellorsville, was an ambitious political general notorious for his explosive temper. While a U.S. Senator from New York before the War, he shot and killed Francis Scott Key's son, who was having an affair with Sickles' wife. At his trial, Sickles pleaded temporary insanity and was acquitted.

west and send just one Signal Corps captain out on picket duty.

In the meantime, General Sickles had requested permission to attack the enemy column moving across his front with his entire corps. Hooker temporized, finally sending word that Sickles was to "advance cautiously toward the road followed by the enemy and harass the movement as much as possible."

But the combative Sickles did far more than that: He assaulted the rear of the Confederate column with two divisions. The attackers drove in the Confederate pickets and overwhelmed the 23rd Georgia Regiment, inflicting 300 casualties. But regiments from Anderson's and A. P. Hill's divisions moved in and held the Federals off. The rest of Jackson's men marched resolutely on.

At this point, Hooker changed his mind again. From the results of the skirmish, and the numbers of ambulances and wagons observed in the enemy column, he jumped to the conclusion that the entire Confederate army was on the move, in which case Lee could only be retreating. The assumption took hold among Hooker's officers on the right flank, and from that time on they blithely ignored the continuing reports of Jackson's approach.

The alarms came thick and fast. At 1 p.m., and again an hour later, Colonel John C. Lee of the 55th Ohio reported to his division commander, Brigadier General Charles Devens, that enemy infantry and artillery were approaching the division's flank on the extreme right of Howard's line. Devens replied that the reports must be false since he had received no information to that effect from corps headquarters.

A short time later, Lieutenant Colonel C.W.F. Friend, another of Devens' officers, came from the division's picket line and reported the Confederate movement to Devens, who again flatly refused to believe it. Friend then went to corps headquarters, where he was upbraided for risking panic with such irresponsible reports.

At about 3 p.m., Colonel Leopold von Gilsa, who commanded Devens' 1st Brigade, received a message from Major Owen Rice of the 153d Pennsylvania — one of the regiments facing west. "A large body of the enemy is massing on my front," read the frantic message. "For God's sake make disposition to receive him!" Von Gilsa took the report to General Howard, who responded angrily that the woods were too thick in Devens' area for an attacker to penetrate.

Captain Hubert Dilger, who commanded

an XI Corps battery, ran into Jackson's column while making a reconnaissance. He was chased by Confederate cavalry and almost captured. Dilger reported his experience at Hooker's headquarters and was told to go peddle his imaginings at XI Corps headquarters. There he was informed that General Lee was in full retreat.

Earlier that afternoon, around 2 p.m., Jackson had ridden to a hill off the Brock Road, at the place where his men were to turn right onto the Orange Plank Road to make their assault. From his vantage point, Jackson could see that the Union right extended farther west than he had thought, and he found himself facing a solid line of entrenchments. Federals were relaxing in the sun, laughing, talking and smoking, some of them lying on their knapsacks. Others were slaughtering beef cattle. Their arms were stacked; all were oblivious to their peril.

Jackson realized at once that in order to turn the Federal flank he first would have to march farther north, to the Turnpike. On a piece of paper held against the pommel of his saddle, he scrawled a message to General Lee: "I hope as soon as practicable to attack. I trust that an ever-kind Providence will bless us with great success."

But it took another two hours for the Confederate columns to reach the Turnpike, close up and form for the assault. The troops deployed in three lines perpendicular to the road and extending a mile on either side of it. Robert Rodes's division was in the front line, with Brigadier General Raleigh Colston's next, and A. P. Hill's in the rear.

Jackson's first objective was the high ground at Taylor's Farm, a thousand yards down the Turnpike. Just beyond the farm,

the Turnpike ran into the Plank Road, which continued east to Chancellorsville. Jackson intended to push down that road and link his right with Lee's divisions around Catherine Furnace; he would also detach a force from his left to take the high ground on Chandler's Farm, north of the Plank Road. From that promontory his artillery would command Chancellorsville and his infantry could block the roads north to Ely's and United States Fords, trapping Hooker's army.

The attackers formed ranks quietly, with orders given in undertones. Shortly after 5 p.m., Jackson turned to General Rodes and asked, "Are you ready?" Rodes calmly answered yes, and the line surged forward.

Seconds after the Confederate attackers stepped off, they were spotted and fired on by startled Federal pickets. The moment the stillness was broken, Confederate bugles blared and the bloodcurdling Rebel yell reverberated through the forest, raising a wave of frightened rabbits, deer and foxes. The attackers dashed forward, ignoring the dense underbrush that ripped their clothes and flesh, and overrunning the Federal pickets.

Then they descended on the astonished men of the 153rd Pennsylvania and 54th New York — the two regiments on Howard's flank that were facing to the west. Remarkably, the Federals were able to leap to their arms, form ranks and fire three volleys, momentarily checking the Confederate advance before giving ground. The two other westernmost regiments — the 41st and 45th New York — were taken in the flank by a murderous fire. They broke for the rear without firing a shot.

One of the few units in the XI Corps not taken by surprise was the 75th Ohio, in re-

Brigadier General Alfred H. Colquitt, a Princeton-educated lawyer and a Methodist minister, commanded a brigade of Georgians in the front line of Jackson's surprise flank attack. When Colquitt halted prematurely to deal with a scattering of Federals on his right, the brigades behind him were blocked; the mistake prevented 3,500 Confederate troops from taking part in the early stages of the fight.

On the afternoon of May 2, Jackson's Confederates, shouting the Rebel yell, storm the Federal breastworks on the Plank Road west of Chancellorsville. The echoes of that wild scream, wrote a Confederate captain, "swept the country for miles."

serve behind the front line. At about 4:30 that afternoon, the regiment's commanding officer, Colonel Robert Reiley, had come to his own conclusion about the reports of the Confederate movement. Highly agitated, he made an impassioned speech to his troops, warning them that a great battle was imminent. "If a comrade falls," he said, "do not stop to take him away or care for him, but fight for the soil on which he falls and save him by victory." Then, telling his men to lie down and rest by their guns, he rode to the front of their line and waited for the onslaught. When it came a half hour later, the regiment, Captain E. R. Monfort wrote, "sprang to arms and deployed into line,"

even as "the two stampeded regiments in our front were rushing through our ranks."

The 75th Ohio opened fire when the oncoming Confederates were only 30 paces away, and kept at it, Monfort related, "until both flanks were overlapped by the enemy, which was bearing down upon them like an avalanche." In the space of 10 minutes Colonel Reiley was slain, his adjutant and 149 other officers and men were killed or wounded, and the rest of the regiment was swept away. After the battle the regimental surgeon, who had remained with the wounded, sent a message through the Confederate lines: "All honor to the 75th; she left her dead and wounded all in line of battle."

In less than an hour, Jackson's men had possession of their first objective, Taylor's Farm. Gaining momentum, they rolled inexorably eastward, driving before them brigade after brigade of the hapless XI Corps.

General Howard was at his headquarters at Dowdall's Tavern on the Plank Road as Jackson approached. Hearing firing off to the west, he rode to a ridge to see what was happening. At first he saw only the rabbits and deer tearing through the woods toward him. But then came the panic-stricken men of his entire 1st Division. "It was a terrible gale," Howard wrote later. "The rush, the rattle, the quick lightning from a hundred points at once; the roar redoubled by the echoes through the forest; the panic, the dead and dying in sight, and the wounded straggling along; the frantic efforts of the brave and patriotic to stay the angry storm."

An aide suggested that Howard fire into the mob to try to stop the terrified soldiers. But Howard refused to fire on his own men. Instead, he grabbed a United States flag and clutched it under the stump of the right arm he had lost earlier in the War at the Battle of Fair Oaks. Then, waving a revolver with his good hand, he shouted over and over, "Halt! Halt! I'm ruined, I'm ruined." His frenzy was so spectacular that Sergeant J. H. Peabody of the 61st Ohio, who was headed for the rear, stopped in amazement and stood amid the chaos, leaning on his musket and, as he sardonically recalled it, "admiring the self-possession of the General."

Just before the rout of XI Corps became complete, one unit managed to make a stand. Colonel Adolphus Buschbeck's brigade had been deployed in reserve in a line of rifle pits at right angles to the Plank Road near Dow-

A Union officer brandishing pistol and saber tries in vain to slow the stampede of the Federal XI Corps down the Plank Road. A lieutenant from Pennsylvania described the retreat as "an avalanche of panic-stricken, flying men, a wild frenzied mob tearing to the rear."

dall's Tavern. There, in the corps's last line of defense, Buschbeck's men managed to delay the Confederate onslaught for half an hour. Volleys delivered by the Federal infantry, along with canister fired by the artillery, "would mow a road clear through them every time," recalled Private James Emmons of the 154th New York. "But they would close up with a yell and come on again." Finally the blue line gave way, and as Emmons put it, "we run, you better believe."

As the Confederate tide swept past Dowdall's Tavern, Sickles' Federals off to the south of Chancellorsville were still unaware of the disaster on the right. Distracted by a demonstration mounted by Lee at Catherine Furnace, Sickles refused to believe an aide to General Howard who brought him the news of the attack to the west. But when it was confirmed, Sickles ordered a cavalry regiment, the 8th Pennsylvania under Major Pennock Huey, to ride to Howard's assistance. Huey's troopers rode down a country lane — straight into Rodes's Confederates.

Although his troopers were surrounded and vastly outnumbered, Huey ordered a charge. "We cut our way through, trampling down all who could not escape us," Huey later recalled. But then a murderous Confederate volley halted the cavalry in its tracks. Major Peter Keenan, commander of Huey's 1st Battalion, went down in a hail of enemy fire, along with the regimental adjutant, 30 men and 80 horses. Thirteen bullets were later counted in Keenan's dead body and nine in the adjutant's lifeless form.

Caught in the same volley, cavalryman John L. Collins had his horse shot out from under him. Collins leaped to his feet and dashed away through the woods as fast as he could run. Gaining the Plank Road, he found himself amid "a scene of terror and confusion such as I had never seen before. Men and animals were dashing against one another in wild dismay before the line of fire that came crackling and crashing after them. The constantly approaching rattle of musketry, the crash of shells through the trees, seemed to come from three sides upon the broken fragments of the Eleventh Corps that crowded each other in the road." Eventually, Collins and other survivors of his regiment would join a new Federal defensive line closer to Chancellorsville.

The ill-fated charge of the 8th Pennsylvania had given Union gunners time to form another line along the Plank Road. Artillery at Hazel Grove joined in the firing, and the barrage began to slow Jackson's advance.

General Hooker, meanwhile, had been sitting on the porch of the Chancellor House

133

Sabers flashing, the 8th Pennsylvania Cavalry charges down a narrow road to assist the beleaguered XI Corps. The gallant Pennsylvanians unwittingly rode straight into Robert Rodes's Confederate division. "We struck it as a wave strikes a stately ship," wrote a cavalryman. "The ship is staggered, but the wave is dashed into spray."

Captain Hubert Dilger, commanding Battery I of the 1st Ohio Artillery, bought time for the remnants of Howard's XI Corps by sweeping the Plank Road with fire until he had only one gun left to slow the rush of grayclad infantry. For this action, Dilger, a German on leave from the army of the Grand Duke of Baden, was awarded the Medal of Honor.

with his aides, Captains William Candler and Harry Russell, enjoying the balmy evening. Because of a freakish atmospheric effect, the uproar of Jackson's attack could not be heard at the Chancellor House.

Suddenly hearing something, Captain Russell leaped to his feet, trained his field glasses up the road and shouted, "My God! Here they come!" Panic-stricken soldiers along with ambulances and wagons burst into view along the Plank Road. Hooker and his aides ran for their horses, galloped up the road directly into the mob, trying in vain to stop the fleeing soldiers.

Hooker remembered that his old III Corps division, now under the command of his good friend, Major General Hiram Berry, was in reserve and close at hand. Extricating himself from the swirling mob, he rode over to Berry and shouted, "General, throw your men into the breach — receive the enemy on your bayonets."

Berry's men formed a line running south from the Plank Road just west of Chancellorsville, and around them Hooker quickly built a new line of defense. More artillery pieces were hurriedly massed at Hazel Grove, and guns were positioned on Fairview Heights, a ridge just south of Chancellor House. A division from XII Corps covered Berry's left flank; stragglers from Howard's corps were sent to form on Berry's right. Along the road running north from Chancellorsville, a brigade of Couch's II Corps troops was posted and ordered to halt any XI Corps fugitives who got that far. A division of Meade's V Corps shifted to cover the northern end of the line, to Couch's right. Meanwhile, troops of General John Reynolds' I Corps, ordered that morning to move toward Chancellorsville, pushed across the river at United States Ford.

As darkness closed in, Jackson's attack began to lose its momentum. In the tangled thickets, officers lost contact with their men, units became scrambled and confused, and the Confederates had no choice but to halt and regroup.

For the past two hours, Stonewall Jackson had been riding forward to urge his men on. "Press on! Press on!" he shouted. And each time wild cries of victory resounded

In this fanciful painting of the battlefield at Chancellorsville, Confederate infantry attacks in the foreground around sunset on May 2. Hooker's Federal troops have

regrouped near Chancellor House *(center)* and have formed a defensive perimeter strengthened by cannon and a charging squadron of cavalry on the Plank Road.

through the forest, he lifted his head and gave thanks to the Lord. At one point a young officer said to Jackson in jest, "General, they are running too fast for us, we can't keep up with them." Jackson turned a stern gaze on the youth and replied, "They never run too fast for me, sir."

Now, as the attack sputtered and a lull descended over the battlefield, Jackson grew impatient. He sent orders to A. P. Hill to move forward, relieve Rodes's weary troops and prepare for a night attack. Then, a little before 9 p.m., Jackson rode ahead with several of his staff officers to scout the enemy lines near the Plank Road.

Moving slowly over the unfamiliar ground in the moonlight, Jackson and his party worked their way close enough to the Federal positions to hear trees being felled and orders being given, then the horsemen turned and started back. As they approached their own lines, pickets of the 18th North Carolina took them for Federal cavalry and opened fire. Several members of the party were shot from their horses. "Cease firing!" shouted Jackson's aide and brother-in-law, Lieutenant Joseph Morrison. "You are firing into your own men!" But a derisive voice answered, "Who gave that order? It's a lie. Pour it into them, boys."

Another volley raked the mounted officers. This time Jackson was hit, taking a bullet in the right hand and two more in his left arm. One ball severed an artery just below the shoulder. Jackson's terrified horse wheeled and bolted into the woods toward the Federal lines; Jackson was struck on the head by branches and almost knocked to the ground, but he managed to rein in the horse with his wounded hand and turn the animal onto the Plank Road.

Bleeding profusely and in great pain, Jackson was helped off his horse and carried to the side of the road. As an aide was ripping the sleeve of Jackson's wounded arm, A. P. Hill rode up. "General," he said, "is the wound painful?"

"Very painful," Jackson replied. "My arm is broken."

A surgeon came up, inspected Jackson's wounds, and saw that the bleeding had slowed. Moving him could start the flow of blood again, but he had to be taken away because a Federal counterattack seemed imminent. Jackson tried to walk but was quickly exhausted.

A litter was brought from the nearby lines and he was persuaded to lie down on it, just as Federal artillery opened up. "Great broadsides thundered over the woods," recalled Captain James Power Smith of Jackson's staff. "Hissing shells searched the dark thickets through, and shrapnels swept the road along which we moved." One of the litter-bearers fell, wounded in both arms; as the litter was lowered, another panicked and ran for safety in the woods. Jackson struggled to rise, but Smith restrained him, saying, "Sir, you must lie still. It will cost you your life if you rise." The barrage thundered on, Smith wrote, "grape-shot striking fire upon the flinty rock of the road all around us, and sweeping from their feet horses and men of the artillery just moved to the front."

When the firing veered away, Smith got Jackson to his feet and they staggered into the protection of the woods. The litter was brought up, and Smith and three others raised it to their shoulders and started again for the rear. They had not gone far when one of them caught a foot in the underbrush and fell headlong. Jackson was thrown to the

Stonewall Jackson sat for this photograph at his headquarters a few days before the fighting began at Chancellorsville. His wife, Mary Anna, visiting with their infant daughter, Julia, persuaded Jackson to have his portrait taken. "I arranged his hair myself, which was unusually long for him, and curled in large ringlets," Mary Anna later wrote. "I never saw him look so handsome and noble." It was the general's last photograph.

ground and landed on his shattered arm. For the first time a groan escaped his lips.

Smith had just got Jackson back on the litter when Brigadier General William Dorsey Pender of A. P. Hill's division appeared. Pender said that the situation was confused and very difficult for the Confederates now: "The lines here are so much broken that I fear we will have to fall back." Jackson was suffering from pain, shock and loss of blood, but those words roused him. "You must hold your ground, General Pender," he growled, "You must hold your ground, sir."

At length the men carrying Jackson found an ambulance, and he was taken to a field hospital at Wilderness Tavern. There Jackson was placed in the care of his friend and corps medical director, Dr. Hunter McGuire. McGuire told him that it might be necessary to amputate the left arm. "Yes, certainly," Jackson answered instantly. "Do for me whatever you think best."

Chloroform was administered and Jackson's left arm was amputated just below the shoulder. About an hour after the operation, while Jackson was still befuddled, Major Alexander "Sandie" Pendleton arrived on an urgent mission. Pendleton was told that he could not see the general, but he insisted that the fate of the army and the Confederate cause itself depended on it. Brought before Jackson, he explained that A. P. Hill, who had taken charge after Jackson was hit, had also been wounded. Jeb Stuart, now in command, wanted to know what he should do.

Jackson struggled to come up with an answer. His brow contracted, and his mouth was set. Finally, he said in a sad, feeble voice, "I don't know; I can't tell. Say to General Stuart he must do what he thinks best."

A Costly Triumph

Despite the spectacular success of Jackson's flanking attack, the Confederates were still far from victory when the battlefield at last fell silent on the night of May 2. Jackson's corps had, in fact, failed to reach two crucial objectives; his right had not been able to link up with Lee's forces north of Catherine Furnace, and his left had been stopped far short of the high ground at Chandler's Farm.

The Federals, hard hit and off balance, spent the night of May 2 frantically reorganizing to stave off another Confederate attack. The new Federal lines formed a loop around Chancellorsville (*map, page 142*), with Couch's II Corps manning the area north of the Plank Road and Slocum's XII Corps deployed to the south. From Slocum's lines, a long, narrow salient manned by Sickles' III Corps jutted southwestward to the high ground at Hazel Grove, about a mile from the Chancellor House.

The Federal troops facing Jackson's forces — the westernmost lines of Couch's and Slocum's corps — had worked feverishly through the night to construct three lines of defense. They had cleared a field of fire about 100 yards wide and used the felled trees and underbrush to erect an abatis behind it. Roughly 100 yards east of the abatis they had put together a solid breastwork of logs. Finally, on the swampy ground at the foot of Fairview Heights, close by Chancellorsville, another wide belt of felled trees and underbrush had been laid down.

The remaining Federal forces were deployed in the outline of a crude V, with its point resting on the top of the Chancellorsville defensive loop and its two sides stretching — one to the northwest, the other to the northeast — all the way to the Rappahannock. The corps of Meade and Reynolds held the northwestern line; Howard's battered corps manned the northeastern wing. Protected within these lines were the roads leading to United States Ford, the Federals' logical route of retreat across the river.

The arrival of Reynolds' corps during the night had brought the Federal strength at Chancellorsville to 76,000 men. They faced 43,000 attackers, who were divided into two wings separated by almost a day's march. The situation demanded a vigorous Federal counterattack, and Hooker had been elevated to the army command because of his reputation as an aggressive combat leader.

But ever since the first contact with the enemy in this campaign, Hooker had been thinking only of defense and the safety of his army, and he showed no inclination to change his posture now. The most he would do this night was send word to General Sedgwick, who was still in his bridgehead below Fredericksburg, to march immediately to Chancellorsville and attack Lee's forces there in the rear. With his 76,000 men, Hooker intended to wait for Sedgwick's force of 23,000 to fight its way to his rescue.

Having thus handed Sedgwick the responsibility and Lee the initiative, Hooker went on to give away another great advantage.

This battle flag, belonging to the 18th Mississippi, was captured on Marye's Heights by Corporal Michael Lamey of the 77th New York on May 3, 1863, during the Chancellorsville Campaign. The New Yorkers then joined in a Federal push west from Fredericksburg.

General Couch remembered it, the development caused Hooker "great alarm, and preparations were at once made to withdraw the whole front, leaving General Sickles to his fate; but that officer showed himself able to take care of his rear, and communication was restored at the point of the bayonet."

Hooker was asleep when Sickles' aide arrived to request reinforcements, and no one would rouse the slumbering general until daybreak. Then, instead of granting the request, the fearful Hooker ordered Sickles to abandon Hazel Grove without delay, to pull his infantry back to new entrenchments nearer the Plank Road and to redeploy his artillery on Fairview Heights. As Sickles grudgingly complied around 6 a.m., Jeb Stuart launched his attack.

A rapid succession of events had thrust Jeb Stuart into command of Stonewall Jackson's corps. When Jackson was wounded, leadership had passed to General A. P. Hill. But within minutes of taking over, Hill himself had been knocked down and so badly bruised by a spent shell fragment that his legs were temporarily paralyzed. He handed over command to the next-senior division officer, General Rodes. But Hill then had second thoughts and, possibly on Jackson's advice, sent for Jeb Stuart to replace Rodes.

This was a highly unusual move; Stuart was a cavalry commander, not an infantry officer. But Hill was more concerned that the venerated Jackson be replaced by a man the troops knew and trusted. Rodes was little known outside his own division, while Stuart was widely admired. Rodes gracefully acquiesced to his instant demotion. As he wrote later, "I was satisfied the good of the service demanded it."

During the night, General Sickles had sent an aide to ask Hooker to reinforce the Federals holding Hazel Grove. This rise jutted between the two wings of Lee's army; Sickles' guns massed there prevented the two Confederate forces from linking and impeded communications between them. Moreover, the hill was an ideal place from which to launch an attack against either enemy wing.

But Sickles' position on Hazel Grove was precarious. The Confederates were pressing him from both sides, and he was in danger of being overrun when the fighting resumed.

Earlier in the evening, in fact, he had been cut off for a time by a Confederate probe. As

All through the night, Stuart reorganized the Confederate lines to prepare for a renewed attack west of Chancellorsville the next morning. Most of Rodes's battered division fell back to Dowdall's Tavern to regroup, and A. P. Hill's division, now commanded by Brigadier General Henry Heth, moved into the front line. General Raleigh Colston's division formed the second line.

Messengers sent by Stuart made the long ride around Sickles' position on Hazel Grove to inform Lee of the latest developments. The commanding general had been shaken by the news of Jackson's wound. "Any victory is a dear one that deprives us of the services of Jackson," he said, "even for a short time." Lee approved of Stuart's moves, but thought it necessary to stress one point. "It is all-important," he wrote to Stuart at 3:30 a.m., "that you continue pressing to the right (toward me), turning, if possible, all the fortified points, in order that we can unite both wings of the army." The key fortified point between the two wings was, of course, Hazel Grove.

Heth's skirmishers moved out early that morning. While most of them were still feeling their way toward the Federal positions through the dewy underbrush, Brigadier General James Archer's brigade on the right, encountering no opposition, advanced up the slopes of Hazel Grove. Archer's men arrived on the crest as the last of Sickles' units were departing. The grayclads rushed forward, captured 100 men and three guns, and gave chase to the retreating Federals.

The Confederates were quick to capitalize on their surprisingly easy conquest. During the night, Colonel E. Porter Alexander had hidden 30 guns in the woods near Hazel Grove. The moment the position was over-run he rushed the batteries onto the heights; soon his guns were pouring a devastating fire on the Federal artillery on Fairview Heights and into Slocum's lines to the east.

Heth's division now descended on the first Federal line of defense across the Plank Road west of Chancellorsville. The attack was preceded by a hellish rain of shot and shell. "Turn right or left, grim death stared at us," wrote one of the defenders, Captain Charles H. Weygant of the 124th New York, in Sickles' corps. "The heavens above seemed filled

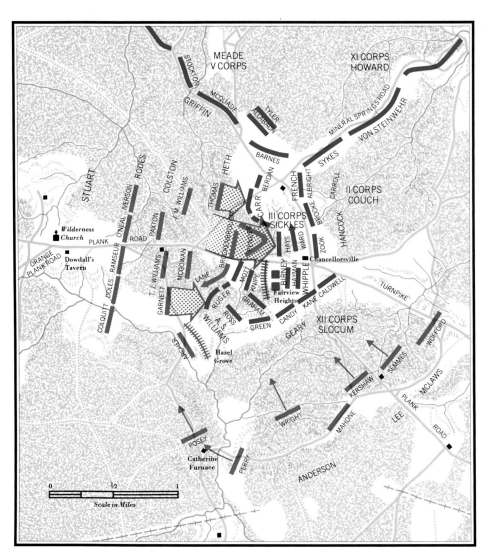

At dawn on May 3, Jeb Stuart's wing of Robert E. Lee's army launched an assault on Joseph Hooker's Federals entrenched west of Chancellorsville. Around 7:30, William Dorsey Pender's brigade of Henry Heth's division broke the Federal line but was driven back. The Confederate attack continued, and Hooker ordered a withdrawal to the area around the Chancellor House. The Confederates pressed their advantage and by noon the Union army was in general retreat toward the Rappahannock.

with hot-breathed, shrieking demons. The knoll beneath us shook like a thing of life. Thick, stifling clouds of smoke rolled back over us, filled with fragments of bursting shells which tore up the ground all around and among us, mangling the bodies of the men who almost covered it." The groans of the dying, Weygant continued, "mingled in horrid discord with the whinnying of wounded beasts and the shrill shouts of those who were continuing the fight."

Units on either side of them disintegrated, but the men of the 124th New York held on. Weygant recorded: "Backward, forward, down, down our brave men fell; thinner and yet thinner grew the ranks, but not a foot of ground was yielded." A shell struck a limber near Weygant and exploded, "turning to blackened corpses nearly a score of men who stood about it." At one point the regiment's colonel, Augustus Van Horne Ellis, rode to the front, and shouting, "Forward, my tulips," led the New Yorkers into the smoke. They stopped the attackers and fought on until their ammunition was exhausted and they were in danger of being flanked on both sides. Only then did the New Yorkers fall back, having lost 204 of their 550 men.

But the Confederate attack was sputtering in places. The order to advance had been given before all of Heth's brigades completed their alignment; as they moved forward through the difficult terrain, gaps developed and widened, and the flanks of brigades became dangerously exposed.

Driving the Federals back south of the Plank Road, Brigadier General Samuel McGowan's South Carolina brigade lost contact with Archer's brigade on Hazel Grove to its right. Brought to a halt before the third Federal line in front of Fairview Heights,

McGowan's men were decimated by musket fire and then driven back by Brigadier General Thomas Ruger's brigade — an avalanche of bluecoats that crashed into McGowan's exposed right flank. As his men retreated, McGowan fell, severely wounded.

The woods themselves posed a terrible threat to the combatants. Exploding artillery shells splintered the trees and sent huge limbs hurtling to the ground to crush or maim unwary soldiers. In several places, the trees and underbrush caught fire and the spreading flames trapped many of the wounded men. "It was pitiful to see the charred bodies hugging the trees, with hands outstretched as if to ward off the flames," said Captain J.F.J. Caldwell of McGowan's brigade. "We saw around them little cleared circles where they had evidently raked away the dead leaves and sticks to stay the progress of the fire."

Shortly before the retreat of McGowan's Confederates, two brigades of North Carolinians under Generals James Lane and William Dorsey Pender had struck the Federal center on either side of the Plank Road. Lane's men, just south of the road, quickly brushed aside a regiment of green Federals, the 3rd Maryland, and overran the log breastwork that constituted the Union's second line. But then Lane's men were checked by two New Jersey regiments, and came under heavy artillery fire from Fairview Heights. At that moment, as McGowan's brigade gave way on the right, the Federals opposite Lane counterattacked and threatened both of his flanks. Lane's command broke apart and was driven back in great confusion. While the survivors were trying to reassemble on the far side of the breastwork, General Ruger's pursuing Federals

caught them milling around and mowed them down at point-blank range.

In the meantime, most of Pender's brigade, deployed just north of the Plank Road, was making no headway against the first Federal line. But one regiment on Pender's left — the 13th North Carolina — managed to link up with Brigadier General Edward L. Thomas' brigade, farther to the north. Together they overran the first two defensive positions and advanced toward Fairview Heights. On the way, the North Carolinians captured a wounded Federal general, William Hays, along with all but one of his staff officers.

The advancing Confederates were on the verge of flanking the Federal guns on Fairview Heights when they ran into stiff resistance from Colonel Emlen Franklin's brigade in their center, combined with a sudden Federal countercharge on their left. This counterthrust was the result of one of Hooker's only aggressive moves of the day. A short time earlier, around 7:30, he had come upon General William French forming a line of battle just off the Plank Road and had ordered French to drive the enemy back. French's men eagerly complied, pushing Thomas' men and the North Carolinians back to the log breastwork and taking several hundred prisoners.

General Hooker's old division, commanded by his friend, General Hiram Berry, had borne the brunt of Pender's and Thomas' advance. Before French's counterattack relieved the pressure, Berry had walked across the Plank Road to confer with one of his brigade commanders. He was halfway back when the crack of a sharpshooter's musket was heard and a wreath of smoke appeared in the foliage of a distant tree. Berry fell to

the road, mortally wounded. "My wife and child," he murmured. "Carry me off the field." In a matter of moments one of Hooker's most trusted officers was dead.

When Hooker saw a group of officers carrying the body from the field, he called out, "Who have you got there, gentlemen?" Told that it was Berry, he jumped down from his horse and bent over the lifeless form. "My God, Berry," he exclaimed. "Why was this to happen? Why was the man on whom I relied so much to be taken in this manner?"

Berry's command passed to Brigadier General Joseph B. Carr. However, Brigadier General Joseph Revere, out of touch with Carr, mistakenly considered himself to be the senior officer in the division. Each man assumed command of a segment of the division. Carr ordered his men to stand their ground. But at the height of the battle, over the protests of his men, Revere

suddenly marched his units — the better part of nine regiments in all — off the field of battle. Revere maintained afterward that the troops needed to be reorganized and resupplied, but his excuse was not accepted. He was tried by a court-martial and sentenced to dismissal from the service — a disgrace President Lincoln later mitigated by allowing him to resign.

Revere was not the only one who failed to meet the test of fortitude and character posed by the terrible arena of the Wilderness. Hooker had deployed two regiments of cavalry behind the lines to stop deserters, and they had a busy day returning to duty fleeing officers and men. Two entire batteries of the demoralized XI Corps galloped for United States Ford on hearing the first sounds of the attack. On the III Corps line, Colonel Louis Francine of the 7th New Jersey became so hoarse from shouting orders that he lost his

145

At the climax of Lee's assault, Colonel E. Porter Alexander *(right)*, commanding the Confederate artillery on the field, poured a devastating fire from 40 guns into the Federal lines. He was credited by Lee with "the successful issue of the contest.'"

voice, and was advised by a surgeon to go to the rear. He did so — taking the 400 survivors of his battered regiment with him.

Yet there were many who stood up to the awful test, some to their own surprise. One soldier of the 20th Connecticut, which was seeing action for the first time, had told his friends quite frankly that he knew he was a coward and would turn tail and run when the shooting started. But the regiment performed admirably, and at the height of the action, the self-professed "coward" was discovered by his captain, calmly loading and firing his weapon. "Hello, Cap'n," he said casually as he bit open a paper cartridge. "I believe the powder goes in fust, don't it?"

In little more than an hour of fighting, Heth's attacking troops had penetrated two of the three Federal defensive positions, but his brigades had then been shattered, separated and driven back. While General Colston's division grimly held on in support of Heth's line, trying to forestall a general retreat, Stuart ordered General Rodes's division to attack.

As Rodes's troops advanced, some Confederate units were retreating, others were moving laterally to plug gaps in the line, and still others were clinging tightly to their hard-won ground. In the smoke and dense brush, Stuart's three lines became hopelessly jumbled and confused — occasionally with tragic results.

On the right, between the Plank Road and Hazel Grove, some of Colston's troops moved up to support McGowan's exhausted brigade. But instead of pushing forward, the men flung themselves to the ground and started firing over the heads of McGowan's troops. Some of the South Carolinians were

Among E. Porter Alexander's most valuable subordinates at Chancellorsville was 25-year-old Major Frank Huger *(left)*, a crack artillerist who commanded six batteries on the strategic hill called Hazel Grove.

wounded, and a young lieutenant was killed, by the fire of the men coming to their relief.

Now McGowan's men and those behind them froze in place, and nothing that their officers could say or do would make any of them move forward. The Stonewall Brigade was ordered down from the left flank to get the advance moving again, and found, in the words of Colonel J.H.S. Funk of the 5th Virginia, "a large number of men of whom fear had taken the most absolute possession."

Federal troops in the area began massing for a counterattack, and Colston ordered the Stonewall Brigade to attack before the Confederates were overrun. As the veterans of Jackson's illustrious Shenandoah Valley Campaign moved up, they disdainfully told

McGowan's men, "We will show you the way to clear a Yankee line." Then, supported by Colonel Thomas S. Garnett's brigade of Virginians, they poured a withering fire into the Federal line and hurled it back. But quickly the tide turned again. Both Garnett and the Stonewall Brigade's commander, Brigadier General Elisha Paxton, were mortally wounded, and before the two brigades had pushed very far they came under a hurricane of fire and were forced to withdraw.

To the north, the brigade commanded by the fiery young North Carolinian, Brigadier General Stephen Dodson Ramseur, came up behind some of Colston's men who were cowering on the ground. Ramseur ordered the soldiers to advance, but not a man moved. Ramseur pleaded and cajoled to no avail. Then he angrily gave his own brigade the order, "Forward, march!" and they clambered over the prostrate soldiers and rushed forward. Colonel Bryan Grimes of the 4th North Carolina furiously stepped on the back of an officer's head and ground the man's face in the dirt.

Ramseur boldly pushed his brigade far out in front, but a gap of nearly 600 yards opened on his right, perilously exposing his flank. He went back twice through the musket and artillery fire, trying in vain to persuade the soldiers of Paxton's, Garnett's and McGowan's brigades to move forward on his right. He sent word to General Rodes that he would have to withdraw unless something was done to protect the exposed flank. Rodes went up to the line and tried his powers of persuasion on the shaken soldiers, but without success.

When Jeb Stuart was informed of the crisis, he galloped up to the Stonewall Brigade, which was lying exhausted on the ground after its earlier attack. The jaunty Stuart, in plumed hat and red-lined cape, rode up and down happily exhorting the men to make yet another effort — singing a parody of a popular song, "Old Joe Hooker, Won't You Come Out of the Wilderness?" Stuart's theatrics and his confident manner turned the trick. The weary men of the Stonewall Brigade, led now by Colonel Funk, pressed forward and closed the gap on Ramseur's right. By this time, however, the exhausted North Carolinians were almost out of ammunition and most of them had to fall back to the log works.

Yet the Stonewall Brigade drove forward, reached the foot of Fairview Heights, and launched an assault against the Federal artillery positioned on the crest. When the attackers got within 100 yards of the batteries, the Federal gunners opened up with canister and cut the Stonewall Brigade to ribbons. One third of the attackers went down. And since no support was forthcoming, the survivors slowly and reluctantly fell back.

General Stuart's attack had as yet achieved no breakthrough, but the assaults had succeeded in wearing the Federals down. The Confederate batteries at Hazel Grove had kept up a relentless fire on the Federal infantry and on the opposing artillery on Fairview Heights. "A glorious day! A glorious day!" exulted 21-year-old Major William Pegram, a Confederate artillery officer at Hazel Grove, and everyone around him shared in the excitement. In one battery, a boy not more than 12 years old was pulling the lanyard on a gun. Every time he yanked it to fire the cannon, he rolled on the ground with joy, to the delight of his older comrades.

At about 9 a.m., French's troops on the Federal right were attacked by two of

Rodes's brigades, under Colonel J. M. Hall and Brigadier General Alfred Iverson. Soon, the Federal line was being driven back on both sides of the Plank Road. The Federal gunners on Fairview Heights, running low on ammunition and threatened with encirclement, abandoned their position, pulling back to a new line closer to Chancellorsville. As the pressure mounted, General Sickles sent his aide, Major Henry E. Tremain, to ask Hooker for reinforcements.

Hooker was standing with his staff on the porch of the Chancellor House when Tremain rode up, and he leaned down over the railing to talk with the young officer. Just then a shell from one of the Confederate batteries at Hazel Grove hit a pillar next to Hooker and split it from end to end. Part of the pillar struck Hooker violently on the head. The commander was knocked senseless, and some of the officers around him thought he was dead.

General Couch, who was next in seniority to Hooker, reached the Chancellor House shortly after the mishap. "The shattered pillar was there," Couch recalled, "but I could not find him nor anyone else. Hurrying through the house, finding no one, my search was continued through the back yard. All the time I was thinking, 'If he is killed, what shall I do with this disjointed army?' Passing through the yard I came upon him, to my great joy, mounted, and with his staff also in their saddles. Briefly congratulating him on his escape — it was no time to blubber or use soft expressions — I went about my own business."

After Couch had left for the front, Hooker, in great pain and with his right side partially paralyzed, rode off for the rear. As Couch put it, "He neither notified me of his going nor did he give any orders to me whatever." As Hooker rode, his pain became more intense. Growing faint, he was helped to the ground, laid on a blanket and given some medicine. After a time he got up again and was starting to remount his horse when a shell from Hazel Grove struck the blanket on which he had been lying. Shaken, Hooker continued on his way. Still he had not relinquished command.

Couch worked feverishly to steady the lines of his II Corps. The Confederates were now within about 500 yards of the Chancellor House. To the north, they threatened to turn the Federal right flank. A portion of the line there was being held by troops under the command of the youthful Colonel Nelson Miles, who had barely recovered from the terrible throat wound he received at Marye's Heights five months before.

Although he had only a handful of understrength regiments at his disposal, Miles had succeeded in holding off several full-scale Confederate assaults. "Tell Colonel Miles he is worth his weight in gold," his division commander, General Hancock, said to an aide. But Miles's luck turned sour. A round fired by a Confederate sharpshooter struck his belt buckle, pierced his stomach, fractured his pelvis and lodged in his thigh. Once again presumed to be dying, he was carried from the field, and his thin line fell back. (The indomitable Miles recovered in time to see action in the Wilderness again, one year later.)

Couch had the 5th Maine Battery brought up to a position just north of Chancellorsville to aid in stemming the Confederate tide. Instead, it was caught in a murderous cross fire. The Confederates now had 30 guns in action on the Federal right, and even

Under a lethal Confederate barrage, soldiers of the Irish Brigade try to salvage a fieldpiece of the 5th Maine Battery while other Union troops retreat *(background)* across the clearing near Chancellor House. "The shells from the Confederate batteries seemed to fill the air," one officer recalled, "tearing up the ground, rending the men and horses limb from limb, blowing up the caissons, exploding and bursting everywhere."

more firing from Fairview Heights and Hazel Grove. Private John F. Chase of the 5th Maine recalled that his battery advanced into "a storm of iron hail." As the gunners galloped into position, Chase wrote later, "the boys were singing: 'I am going home, to die no more,' and in less than thirty minutes half of our number had 'gone home.' Even before we could get into position our horses and men went down like grass before the scythe." Soon all of the 5th Maine's officers had been wounded and all but two of the guns had been put out of commission.

Couch believed that the Federals could still save the day if he found a way to counterattack. But this was not to be. Around 9:30 a.m., he received a summons from Hooker. Couch found the commanding general lying in a tent near the Chandler House, half a mile north of Chancellorsville. Hooker raised himself up a bit and said, "Couch, I turn the command of the army over to you." But Couch was only to command a retreat, for Hooker produced a map and ordered the army withdrawn to the north, closer to the Rappahannock. Hooker would still make the big decisions for his army.

When Couch emerged from the tent, General Meade and others who were there waiting for instructions expected that the army would go over the attack at last. They were bitterly disappointed to learn differently.

As the first Federal units headed for the rear, the 5th Maine Battery was still firing, although by now it had only one gun. Lieutenant Edmund Kirby, who had taken charge of what was left, was hit by a shell that almost severed his leg. The two remaining gunners fired canister at the approaching Confederates until a shell struck their weapon in the muzzle, disabling it. Private Chase then asked the wounded lieutenant for permission to carry him from the field. "No," Kirby responded, "not until the guns are taken off." And only after all the guns had been dragged away by infantrymen — the battery's horses had all been killed — would Kirby consent to be carried off. Before he died a month later, Kirby was promoted to brigadier general by the President.

With General Hancock's division as a rear guard, the Federals withdrew to a new perimeter north of Chancellorsville. The line — an arc with both ends anchored on the river — was completed by noon. At about that time, General Lee, whose divisions had at last linked up with Stuart's forces, rode into the clearing at the Chancellorsville crossroads, where the Chancellor House was burning furiously. Major Charles Marshall, one of Lee's staff officers, recalled the scene: "The fierce soldiers, with their faces blackened by the smoke of battle, the wounded, crawling with feeble limbs from the fury of the devouring flames, all seemed possessed of a common impulse. One long, unbroken cheer, in which the feeble cry of those who lay helpless on the earth blended with the strong voices of those who still fought, hailed the presence of the victorious chief."

As Lee watched the flames devour the Chancellor House, taking a moment to savor his triumph, a message arrived from Stonewall Jackson. Jackson simply confirmed that he had been wounded and congratulated Lee on the victory. But the staff officer who read the note to Lee saw anguish

Colonel Nelson Miles skillfully commanded a skirmish line of II Corps troops that covered Hooker's retreat to the Chancellor House plateau. After repulsing several enemy assaults, Miles suffered a wound that put him out of the battle. His brigade commander reported, "I know of no terms of praise too exaggerated to characterize his masterly ability."

on his face, and heard his voice tremble as he dictated a reply: "Could I have directed events, I should have chosen for the good of the country to be disabled in your stead. I congratulate you upon the victory, which is due to your skill and energy."

Lee was about to press the attack northward when he was distracted by a messenger bringing news from Fredericksburg: General Sedgwick was on the move.

Hooker's orders to Sedgwick — to cross the Rappahannock at Fredericksburg late on the night of May 2 and march at once to Chancellorsville — had reflected a complete misunderstanding of Sedgwick's situation. Hooker seemed not to know that Sedgwick had long since crossed the river below Fredericksburg, and the Federal commander was under the erroneous impression that there were virtually no Confederate troops left in Fredericksburg. Not surprisingly, therefore, Sedgwick was dumfounded when he received the orders at about 11 p.m. on May 2.

To follow the orders literally would be absurd. Sedgwick would have to recross the river below Fredericksburg that night, move north, throw bridges across at the town under fire, smash through Jubal Early's defenses, and only then take up the march for Chancellorsville. And Hooker expected him to attack the rear of Lee's army at dawn.

Sedgwick decided to follow the spirit, not the letter, of his orders. He would take the most direct route toward Chancellorsville — the Old Richmond Road north from his bridgehead into Fredericksburg, then the Plank Road west toward Lee. This movement had nothing to recommend it; to gain the Plank Road, Sedgwick would be forced to advance up Marye's Heights, attacking

During the gradual withdrawal of Hooker's forces north from the Chancellorsville crossroads, a Federal battle line braves the onslaught of Jeb Stuart's men. "The crash of the musketry was deafening," recalled Sergeant Rice Bull of the 123rd New York. "We loaded and fired as fast as possible, but still they came on."

Major General Winfield Scott Hancock demonstrated both military skill and great bravery as overall commander of the rear guard that covered the Federal withdrawal on May 3. His corps commander, General Darius Couch, trusted Hancock completely; Couch's only order to Hancock was simply, "Take care of things."

the very stone wall on which the Army of the Potomac had been smashed in December. But it seemed the only way that Sedgwick could obey his commanding general.

General John Gibbon, still at Falmouth, was ordered to lay a bridge across the river at Fredericksburg and join Sedgwick there before dawn on May 3. Now history began to repeat itself with terrible exactitude. The Confederate riflemen in Fredericksburg — the same Mississippi units that had so effectively delayed Burnside's crossing there in December — had enough moonlight to shoot by, and they stopped Gibbon's first attempt cold. Gibbon decided to wait until dawn.

At 2:35 a.m. on May 3, Sedgwick received a message from General Daniel Butterfield, Hooker's chief of staff: "Everything in the world depends upon the rapidity and promptness of your movement. Push everything." Around 4 a.m., a follow-up message from Hooker grandly informed Sedgwick that the forces facing him were negligible and must not be allowed to slow his advance.

In fact, Early had 9,000 men at his disposal. They were spread thin but backed by 56 guns, and the works on Marye's Heights were more formidable than ever. A week earlier Major Sandie Pendleton of Jackson's staff had written in awe of the "long lines of trenches and the redoubts which crown every hillside from ten miles above Fredericksburg to twenty miles below. The world has never seen such a fortified position."

Despite continual harassment by Confederate skirmishers, Sedgwick's corps reached Fredericksburg by about 5 a.m., and in the first light of dawn he directed General John Newton, whose division had led the march, to make a reconnaissance toward the stone wall at the foot of Marye's Heights. Newton's troops were hurled back by a storm of shot and shell as Sedgwick watched glumly from horseback. "By Heaven, sir," he said to an aide, "This must not delay us."

By now Gibbon's division was crossing the river, and Sedgwick ordered him to assault the Confederate line to the right of the stone wall while the division under Brigadier General Albion Howe attacked to the left. Meanwhile, Newton, commanding his own and

Colonel Hiram Burnham's divisions, would demonstrate against the center. Under constant artillery fire from Marye's Heights, the troops took up their positions and began the advance around 10 a.m.

The movement immediately foundered. The Federals had neglected to consider a couple of key terrain features in the path of their attack. Gibbon's entire division slowed to a crawl at the canal that crossed the plain just outside town, and quickly came under withering artillery fire. Howe's division, meanwhile, became ensnarled on the left in the deep gully formed by Hazel Run. The only option seemed to be a frontal assault on the stone wall by Newton's divisions.

At least the Federal commanders now remembered the bitter lessons learned during Sumner's ill-fated attacks over the same ground. Instead of forming in lines of battle — the tactic that had proved so costly before — 10 of Newton's regiments were deployed in two columns for the attack. There were 4,700 men in all. And they were told not to stop and fire but to advance at the double-quick with unloaded muskets and rely on the bayonet to clear the Sunken Road.

When the Federals had trotted to within 300 yards of the stone wall, a pair of Confederate howitzers firing canister obliterated the leading ranks of the right column. The left column pressed forward to within 50 yards of the wall, and then all at once a sheet of flame and a hail of lead leaped out from the defenders' muskets. The column staggered and reeled back. Cries of "Retreat!" were heard, but then other voices shouted, "Don't go back! We shan't get so close again." The column surged forward, but wavered in the face of the devastating fire. Finally the men fell back and took cover.

The 7th Massachusetts took refuge behind a high board fence around a house. Peering at the Confederate position through the fence, the men thought they spotted a section near the end of the wall that was lightly held. A party of stretcher-bearers sent out under a flag of truce confirmed that the stone wall was indeed vulnerable on the right. Impulsively, with a shout of "Massachusetts colors to the front!" the men of the 7th swarmed out from behind the fence and toward the wall. On their left Colonel Thomas Allen of the 5th Wisconsin instructed his men to attack with bayonets, galvanizing them with his exhortation: "When the signal 'forward' is given, you will start at double-quick, you will not fire a gun, and you will not stop until you get the order to halt. You will never get that order."

The men sprang up, charged forward, cleared the stone wall in fierce hand-to-hand fighting and went rushing on up the hill. All of Newton's regiments now joined in the attack, sweeping up Marye's Heights and capturing six guns from the Washington Artillery. Gaining the crest, they saw Early's soldiers, wagons, horses and artillery pieces dashing off along the Telegraph Road to the south. Sedgwick did not bother to pursue them, but concentrated on starting his column toward Chancellorsville as ordered, leaving some of Gibbon's troops to hold the heights. It was 11 a.m., and Sedgwick was six hours behind schedule.

At Chancellorsville, General Lee dispatched McLaws' division eastward to intercept Sedgwick. McLaws' four brigades marched to the Salem Church, about four miles west of Fredericksburg, and there formed a line on the edge of a wood. They were joined by five regiments of Alabama infantry under Brigadier General Cadmus Wilcox, who had sent some of his men ahead to skirmish with Sedgwick's lead elements. The Confederates in the vicinity numbered 10,000.

Sedgwick, a brave but methodical general, was so slow in getting his divisions moving toward Chancellorsville from Marye's Heights that General Butterfield talked of relieving him three different times. But nothing was done, and Sedgwick was still in command when his vanguard approached Salem Church at about 3:30 p.m.

The Confederate regiments were deployed on both sides of the Plank Road; just south of the road one company of the 9th Alabama occupied a schoolhouse and another held the

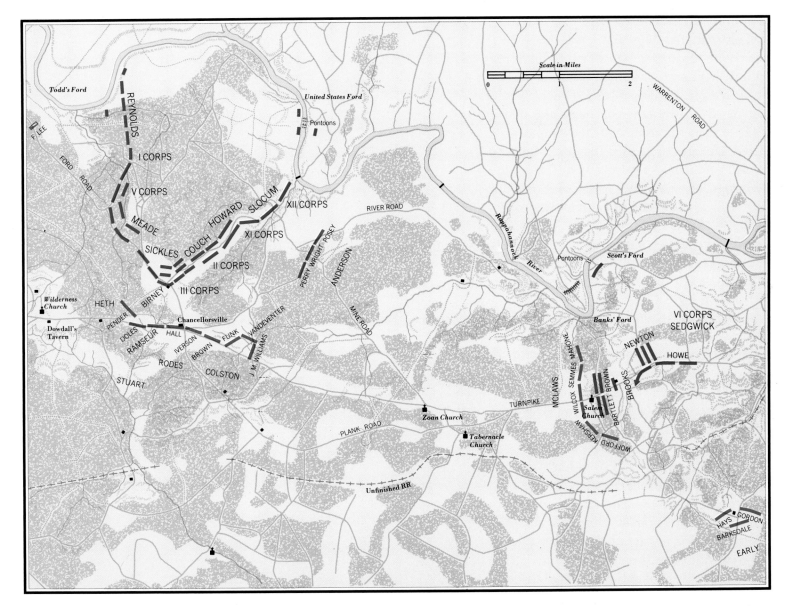

On the afternoon of May 3, the Confederate forces faced the numerically superior Federals on two fronts more than six miles apart. In heavy fighting at Salem Church, 10,000 troops under McLaws halted the advance of Sedgwick's VI Corps from Fredericksburg. Meanwhile, Lee's main force of 25,000 men confronted Hooker's 75,000 men north of Chancellorsville.

church. After driving back Wilcox's skirmishers, Sedgwick's men charged the Confederate position and came under heavy fire. Their lines wavered, but the men kept moving. Soldiers of the 23rd New Jersey and 121st New York surrounded the schoolhouse and captured the defenders there. The Confederate line was broken, and a Federal victory appeared imminent. But then Wilcox

hurled the eight remaining companies of the 9th Alabama into the battle. The Alabamians drove back the Federal line and recaptured the school, freeing the prisoners. When three more Alabama regiments swept forward, the Federals broke for the rear.

Sedgwick had launched his attack aggressively, but he had used only one division — 4,000 men of the 19,000 in his command.

Two fresh divisions arrived in time to stabilize his shattered lines. But it was too late in the day to organize a new attack. "We slept in line that night with the dead of the day's battle lying near us," wrote Lieutenant Colonel Martin T. McMahon of Sedgwick's staff. "The stretcher bearers with their lamps wandered here and there over the field, and the loaded ambulances rattled dismally over the broken plank road. The pickets were unusually still, for the men of both armies were tired, and went willingly to rest. The night was inexpressibly gloomy."

Lee was so confident that Hooker was not going to attack that he ordered Anderson's division to leave Chancellorsville and reinforce McLaws at Salem Church. Early's division, which had withdrawn to a position 4 miles southwest of Fredericksburg, was ordered to reoccupy the town. This left only 25,000 men — the three divisions of Jackson's old corps — to keep watch on Hooker's 75,000. But Lee had taken Hooker's measure by now and thought the risk small.

On the morning of May 4, Early drove Gibbon's pickets from the high ground behind Fredericksburg. He left General William Barksdale's brigade there to watch the Federals in the town, and set out for Salem Church with the rest of his division.

By the middle of the morning, Lee had arrived at Salem Church to take command of the three Confederate divisions — 21,000 men — that were converging there. Sedgwick, meanwhile, had shifted his 19,000 troops northward toward the Rappahannock, forming them in the shape of a horseshoe to cover his line of retreat over Scott's Mill Ford. There Hooker's chief engineer, Brigadier General Henry Benham, had supervised the construction of two pontoon

bridges in case the Federals had to withdraw.

Lee intended to destroy Sedgwick's force. Early was to attack from the east and push the defenders before him into the path of Anderson, who would advance from the south, and McLaws, who would press from the west. Meanwhile, Lee's artillery would destroy the two bridges, and Brigadier General John B. Gordon's brigade would advance along the river to Early's right.

It was 5:30 p.m. before everyone got into position for the attack. Two brigades of Early's division pushed westward as planned, throwing the 20th New York and an artillery battery back in confusion. But instead of marching north as intended, Anderson moved to the right, toward the sounds of battle, to join in Early's attack. Some of the Confederate units became entangled in the thick underbrush and started firing at each other, even as Federal resistance stiffened; the attackers had to pull back and regroup. Gordon did manage to drive back the Federal skirmishers on his front, but was halted when he reached the main enemy line. McLaws' troops advanced on the left through dense woods, but unaccountably failed to make contact with the enemy.

Though the Confederates had not broken through his perimeter, Sedgwick decided around 6:45 p.m. to pull his lines in closer to the river. All the while, the Confederate gunners kept up their barrage. The pontoon bridges at Scott's Mill Ford remained intact, but Sedgwick was worried. Shortly before midnight he sent a message to Hooker: "If I had only this army to care for, I would withdraw it tonight. Do your operations require that I should jeopardize it by retaining it here? An immediate reply is indispensable, or I may feel obliged to withdraw."

Sedgwick was obviously in trouble. But Hooker, snug in his entrenchments, had not even probed the weak enemy line in front of him and felt no obligation to assist the outnumbered and beleaguered force he had ordered to come to his relief. Throughout the evening of the 4th he had listened to the guns pounding Sedgwick and done nothing, even though some of his subordinates had begged to be allowed to attack.

At midnight, Hooker summoned his corps commanders to a council of war. Meade, Howard, Reynolds, Couch and Sickles were present; Slocum, whose corps was farthest from Hooker's headquarters, did not arrive until the meeting was over.

Hooker posed the question: Should they withdraw across the river, or fight it out on the south side of the Rappahannock? After much discussion, Meade, Reynolds and Howard voted to attack. Sickles favored withdrawal, and Couch — who actually wanted to attack, but had no confidence in Hooker — reluctantly sided with Sickles.

Once the vote was taken, Hooker blithely ignored it and gave orders for the entire army, Sedgwick included, to withdraw across the river. Hooker was among the first over the Rappahannock, leaving the details of the complicated and dangerous retreat to his corps commanders. An angry Reynolds exclaimed to his fellow officers, "What was the use of calling us together at this time of night when he intended to retreat anyhow?"

Once again the Army of the Potomac showed more skill in retreat than it had in battle. At 5 a.m. that morning, May 5, Sedgwick reported that his troops were across the river and that the bridges at Scott's Mill Ford had been dismantled. It took the main body of the army to the west much longer. New

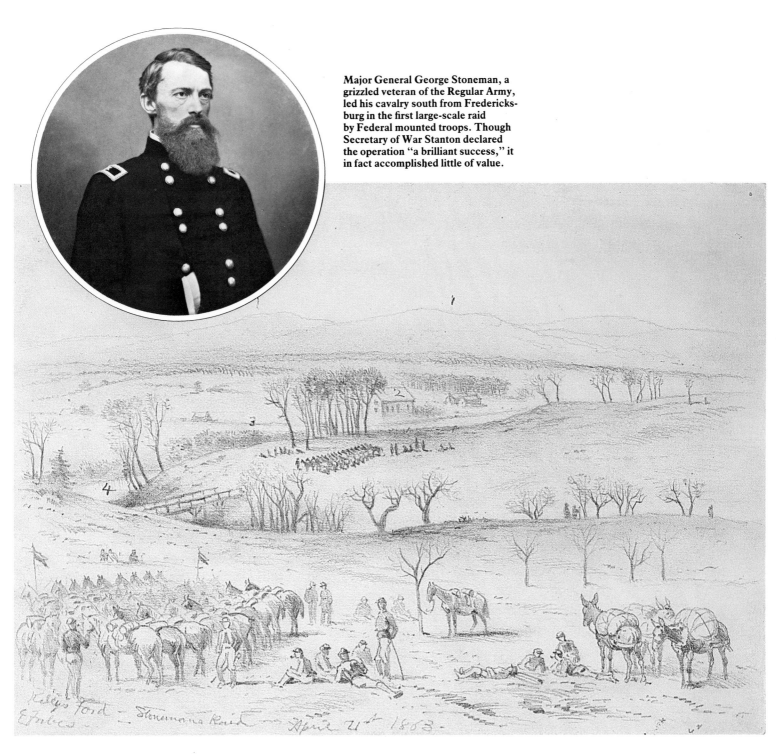

Major General George Stoneman, a grizzled veteran of the Regular Army, led his cavalry south from Fredericksburg in the first large-scale raid by Federal mounted troops. Though Secretary of War Stanton declared the operation "a brilliant success," it in fact accomplished little of value.

On April 21, troopers of Stoneman's cavalry corps rest on the hills north of the Rappahannock, waiting for the rain-swollen river to subside. Bad weather delayed the launching of their raid toward Richmond for more than a week and hampered operations throughout. Cavalry Captain George Sanford recalled, "From the 15th of April until the 8th of May I doubt whether my clothes were ever dry."

roads had to be cut through the Wilderness to the crossing point at United States Ford. It rained hard during the day, and that night the river rose, submerging the ends of the three pontoon bridges at the ford. One bridge had to be dismantled to extend the other two, and the crossing was completed on the morning of May 6.

The exhausted and dispirited army returned to Falmouth, and Stoneman's cavalry straggled back from its raid to the south shortly afterward. Stoneman's horsemen had severed some enemy rail lines and destroyed supply depots, and they had ridden within two miles of Richmond, frightening the population. But Hooker was dismayed that the cavalry had done little to affect the outcome of the Chancellorsville Campaign.

In the days that followed, Hooker did his best to shift responsibility to others and to present the debacle in the best possible light. A message from Butterfield informing President Lincoln of the withdrawal reflected Hooker's interpretation of events: "The Cavalry have failed in executing their orders. General Sedgwick failed in the execution of his orders." The President was horrified to learn that the Army of the Potomac had been defeated yet again. "My God! My God!" he exclaimed. "What will the country say?"

Hooker issued an order commending the army, saying that more could not have been accomplished under the circumstances, and adding: "Whenever we have fought, we have inflicted heavier blows than we have received." But the men were not fooled. "The wonder of the private soldiers was great," wrote Private Warren Goss. "How had one half of the army been defeated while the other half had not fought? The muttered curses were prolonged and deep as they plodded back in the mud to their old camps."

"At Chancellorsville we gained another victory," General Lee said later. "Our people were wild with delight. I, on the contrary, was more depressed than after Fredericksburg; our losses were severe, and again we had gained not an inch of ground, and the enemy could not be pursued." The Battle of Chancellorsville would come to be known as Lee's masterpiece, an almost perfect example of the military arts. But while inflicting 17,000 casualties on the enemy, the Confederates had suffered 13,000 themselves, and the resources of the South were strained to the point where losses of that magnitude could no longer be sustained.

What is more, the Army of Northern Virginia had suffered a disproportionate number of casualties among its high command —

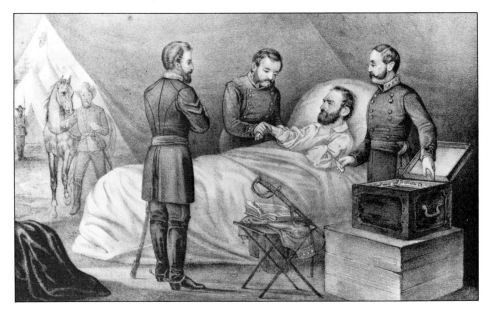

division commanders A. P. Hill and Henry Heth, 11 brigade commanders, including Dorsey Pender, and 40 regimental commanders. Overshadowing all of these, of course, was the loss of corps commander Stonewall Jackson.

On the morning of May 5, Jackson was taken to a field hospital at Guinea Station, about 10 miles south of Fredericksburg, and seemed to be recovering from the amputation of his arm. But Jackson had developed a severe cold, and early on the morning of May 7, he complained of nausea and a pain in his abdomen. His surgeon, Dr. Hunter McGuire, was awakened, and diagnosed pneumonia of the right lung, an illness for which there was no medical help.

Lee was informed of Jackson's sudden turn for the worse, but refused to admit that Jackson's illness might be fatal. "Tell him to make haste and get well, and come back to me as soon as he can," Lee said. "He has lost his left arm, but I have lost my right."

On Sunday, May 10, Jackson's wife told

This fanciful engraving of the death of Stonewall Jackson shows him succumbing to his wound in a tent rather than in the small house near Guinea Station where he actually died. When news of Jackson's death was released, wrote Major Henry Kyd Douglas, "a great sob swept over the Army of Northern Virginia. It was the heart-break of the Southern Confederacy."

her husband that the doctor did not think he would live through the day. "Very good, it is all right," he said, adding that he had always wanted to die on a Sunday. "It will be an infinite gain to be translated to heaven." His mind seemed to wander then. He shouted orders to subordinates, instructing A. P. Hill to prepare for action. In midafternoon, while the room was filled with bright spring sunshine, he said in a firm but quiet voice: "Let us cross over the river and rest under the shade of the trees." And he died.

Lee immediately issued General Order No. 61: "With deep regret the commanding general announces the death of Lieutenant-General T. J. Jackson. Let his name be a watch-word to his corps who have followed him to victory on so many fields. Let his officers and soldiers emulate his invincible determination to do everything in the defense of our loved Country."

Jackson's remains were taken to Richmond and lay in state at the Confederate Capitol. All the city's businesses were closed, and crowds of tearful mourners came to gaze at his coffin. The body was then removed to Lexington, where he had taught at the Virginia Military Institute before the War, and there he was laid to rest in the shade of the trees.

In this photograph mounted on cardboard, cadets of the Virginia Military Institute's class of 1868 gather at Stonewall Jackson's grave near the campus to honor the hero and former VMI professor — a custom followed yearly by the students for decades after the War. Announcing Jackson's death, the institute's superintendent, Francis Smith, said: "Our loss is distinctive. He was peculiarly our own."

Occupying the buttress of a wrecked railroad bridge that had spanned the Rappahannock at Fredericksburg, pickets of Brigadier General William Barksdale's Mississippi Brigade stare across the river at Union positions during the informal truce before the Battle of Chancellorsville. In this rare photograph of enemy troops, the camera lens has somewhat foreshortened the 400-foot distance between Russell and the Confederates.

The War at Close Range

As the Chancellorsville Campaign commenced late in April 1863, a photographer named Andrew J. Russell took a series of pictures — seen here and on the following pages — that come nearer to showing actual combat than any other Civil War photographs. No camera of the time, including Russell's, was capable of capturing men in motion, but his photographs were taken perilously close to the action — some within range of enemy muskets.

Russell was the War's only official Army photographer. A captain in the 141st Volunteers, a unit recruited in his native upstate New York, he was detached from the regiment to document with his camera the construction of military railroads. This assignment took him to the outskirts of Fredericksburg as Major General John Sedgwick's VI Corps prepared to attack toward Chancellorsville.

Once in the battle zone, Russell seized the chance to photograph Federal artillerymen and infantrymen readying for the assault, and even some of the waiting enemy (right). Then he boldly followed Sedgwick's advancing regiments across the Rappahannock and up the formidable heights beyond Fredericksburg, recording unforgettable scenes of carnage and destruction — and narrowly escaping a Confederate counterattack. Russell's reward: pictures that recorded the face of war as the soldiers saw it.

A photograph taken by Russell on Stafford Heights shows the gunners of Captain Franklin A. Pratt's Battery M, 1st Connecticut Heavy Artillery, as they prepare to

bombard Confederate positions across the Rappahannock below Fredericksburg. The battery was armed with 4.5-inch rifled siege guns.

Men of the 15th New York Engineers gather around a pot of stew on the Confederate side of the Rappahannock after completing pontoon bridges (*background*) about a mile below Fredericksburg. Photographer Russell had crossed the Rappahannock on the heels of advance units of Sedgwick's VI Corps that were positioning themselves for the assault.

A pair of Union officers standing just beyond musket range survey Confederate positions southwest of Fredericksburg while their troops take cover in captured rifle pits behind the Old Richmond Road. The infantry in the foreground are New Jersey troops from the 1st Brigade of Brigadier General William Brooks's division. Guns of Battery D, 2nd U.S. Artillery, can be seen in the background. In the assault on May 3, these troops would advance past Marye's Heights, only to suffer a bloody repulse at nearby Salem Church.

Confederate dead of the 18th Mississippi sprawl in the Sunken Road on Marye's Heights, where repeated Union attacks during the first battle at Fredericksburg had been stopped cold. Russell took this picture on May 4, the day after the successful Union attack.

Brigadier General Herman Haupt (*below, left*), the field commander of the U.S. Military Railroads, and one of his assistants, William Wright, survey a wrecked caisson and dead horses left behind by the Washington Artillery of New Orleans. The two men explored the battlefield with Russell on May 4, the same day that Jubal Early retook Marye's Heights; Haupt and Russell narrowly escaped capture.

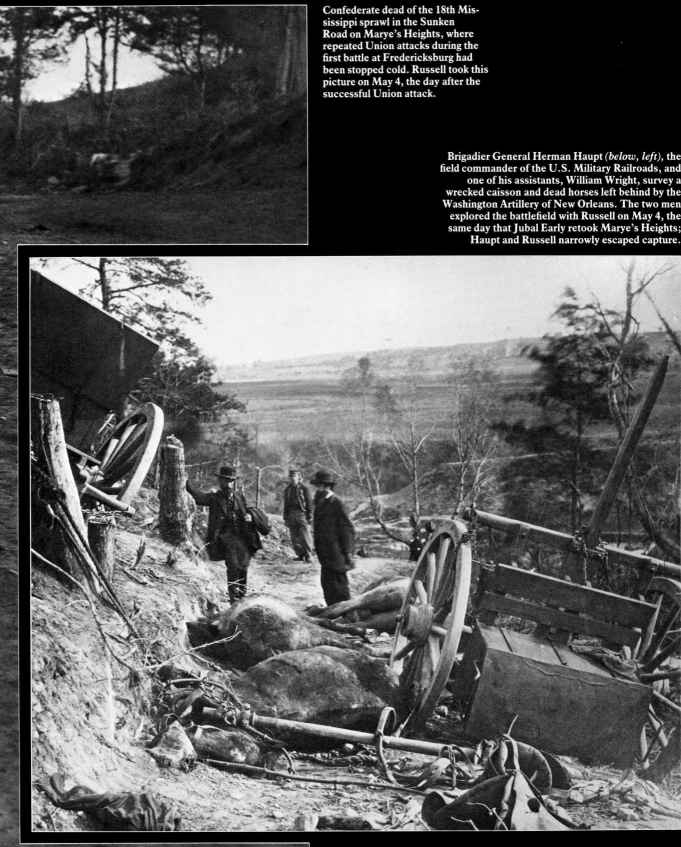

ACKNOWLEDGMENTS

The editors wish to thank the following individuals and institutions for their valuable assistance in the preparation of this volume:

California: San Marino — Brita F. Mack, Photo Archives, Rare Books Department, Huntington Library.

Maryland: Clinton — William Turner.

Massachusetts: Cambridge — Jennie Rathbun, Houghton Library, Harvard University.

Mississippi: Jackson — Anne Lipscomb, Mary Lohrenz, State of Mississippi Department of Archives and History. Oxford — Martha Cofield.

Ohio: Cleveland — Mary Brooke, Charles Sherrill, Western Reserve Historical Society Library.

Pennsylvania: Carlisle — A. Pierce Bounds; Randy Hackenburg, Michael J. Winey, U.S. Army Military History Institute. Gettysburg — Larry Eckert, Gettysburg National Military Park Museum. Harrisburg — Richard A. Sauers, Pennsylvania Capitol Preservation Committee. Philadelphia — Russ Pritchard, War Library and Museum of the Military Order of the Loyal Legion of the United States. West Chester — Harry Roach, *Military Images Magazine.*

Rhode Island: Providence — Richard Harrington, Anne S. K. Brown Military Collection, Brown University Library; Ted Sanderson, Rhode Island Historical Preservation Commission; Phyllis Silva, Rhode Island State Archives.

Texas: Austin — Lawrence T. Jones.

Virginia: Alexandria — Susan Cumbey, Wanda Dowell, Walton Owen, Fort Ward Museum. Falls Church — Chris Nelson. Fredericksburg — Robert K. Krick, David Lilley, Edmund Raus, Fredericksburg-Spotsylvania National Military Park. Lexington — June Cunningham, Virginia Military Institute Museum. McLean — Thomas G. Mays Jr. Richmond — David Hahn, Museum of the Confederacy; Sarah Shields, Valentine Museum.

Washington, D.C.: Eveline Nave, Photoduplication Service, Library of Congress; Jerome Kearns, Prints and Photographs, Library of Congress; Barbara Burger, Bobbeye West, Still Pictures Branch, National Archives; Ted Alexander, National Capital Parks East.

Wisconsin: Howard Madaus, Milwaukee Public Museum.

The index for this book was prepared by Nicholas J. Anthony.

BIBLIOGRAPHY

Books

Alexander, E. P., *Military Memoirs of a Confederate: A Critical Narrative*. Dayton: Morningside Bookshop, 1977.

Alexander, Ted, ed., *The 126th Pennsylvania*. Shippensburg, Pennsylvania: Beidel Printing House, 1984.

Allan, William, *The Army of Northern Virginia in 1862*. Boston: Houghton, Mifflin, 1892.

Averell, William Woods, *Ten Years in the Saddle*. Ed. by Edward K. Eckert and Nicholas J. Amato. San Rafael, California: Presidio Press, 1978.

Bates, Samuel P., *The Battle of Chancellorsville*. Meadville, Pennsylvania: Edward T. Bates, 1882.

Bigelow, John, Jr., *The Campaign of Chancellorsville*. New Haven: Yale University Press, 1910.

Brainard, Mary Genevie Green, comp., *Campaigns of the One Hundred and Forty-sixth Regiment, New York State Volunteers*. New York: G. P. Putnam's Sons, 1915.

Bull, Rice C., *Soldiering: The Civil War Diary of Rice C. Bull, 123rd New York Volunteer Infantry*. Ed. by K. Jack Bauer. San Rafael, California: Presidio Press, 1977.

Caldwell, J.F.J., *History of a Brigade of South Carolinians, Known First as "Gregg's," and Subsequently as "McGowan's Brigade."* Philadelphia: King & Baird, 1866.

Carter, Robert Goldthwaite, *Four Brothers in Blue*. Austin: University of Texas Press, 1978.

Catton, Bruce:
The Army of the Potomac: Glory Road. Garden City: Doubleday, 1952.
Never Call Retreat. Garden City: Doubleday, 1965.

Child, William, *A History of the Fifth Regiment, New Hampshire Volunteers, in the American Civil War, 1861-1865*. Bristol, New Hampshire: R. W. Musgrove, 1893.

Commager, Henry Steele, ed., *The Blue and the Gray: The Story of the Civil War as Told by Participants*. Vol. 1. New York: New American Library, 1973.

Conyngham, David Power, *The Irish Brigade and Its Campaigns*. New York: William McSorley, 1867.

Corby, William, *Memoirs of Chaplain Life*. Notre Dame: "Scholastic" Press, 1894.

Dana, Charles A., *Recollections of the Civil War*. New York: D. Appleton, 1902.

Davenport, Alfred, *Camp and Field Life of the Fifth New York Volunteer Infantry*. New York: Dick and Fitzgerald, 1879.

Dickert, D. Augustus, *History of Kershaw's Brigade*. Dayton: Morningside Bookshop, 1976.

Favill, Josiah Marshall, *The Diary of a Young Officer Serving with the Armies of the United States during the War of the Rebellion*. Chicago: R. R. Donnelley, 1909.

Frassanito, William A., *Grant and Lee: The Virginia Campaigns, 1864-1865*. New York: Charles Scribner's Sons, 1983.

Freeman, Douglas Southall:
Lee's Lieutenants: A Study in Command. Vol. 2. New York: Charles Scribner's Sons, 1943.
R. E. Lee: A Biography. Vol. 2. New York: Charles Scribner's Sons, 1934.

Gibbon, John, *Personal Recollections of the Civil War*. Dayton: Morningside Bookshop, 1978.

Hassler, Warren W., Jr., *Commanders of the Army of the Potomac*. Baton Rouge: Louisiana State University Press, 1962.

Haupt, Herman, *Reminiscences of General Herman Haupt*. New York: Arno Press, 1981 (reprint of 1901 edition).

Hebert, Walter H., *Fighting Joe Hooker*. Indianapolis: Bobbs-Merrill, 1944.

Henderson, G.R.R., *Stonewall Jackson and the American Civil War*. New York: Longmans, Green, 1909.

Hitchcock, Frederick L., *War from the Inside: The Story of the 132nd Regiment Pennsylvania Volunteer Infantry in the War for the Suppression of the Rebellion, 1862-1863*. Philadelphia: J. B. Lippincott, 1904.

Huey, Pennock, *A True History of the Charge of the Eighth Pennsylvania Cavalry at Chancellorsville*. Philadelphia: Porter & Coates, 1883.

Jackson, Mary Anna, *Life and Letters of General Thomas J. Jackson*. New York: Harper & Brothers, 1892.

Johnson, Robert Underwood, and Clarence Clough Buel, eds., *Battles and Leaders of the Civil War: Retreat from Gettysburg*. New York: Castle Books, 1956.

Jones, Paul John, *The Irish Brigade*. Washington: Robert B. Luce, 1969.

Lanier, Richard Nunn, *The Angel of Marye's Heights*. Fredericksburg: Fredericksburg Press, 1961.

Locke, William Henry, *The Story of the Regiment (11th Pennsylvania Volunteers)*. Philadelphia: J. B. Lippincott, 1868.

Longstreet, James, *From Manassas to Appomattox: Memoirs of the Civil War in America*. Bloomington: Indiana University Press, 1960.

McClellan, Carswell, *General Andrew A. Humphreys at Malvern Hill, Va., July 1, 1862, and at Fredericksburg, Va., December 13, 1862*. St. Paul, 1888.

Massey, Mary Elizabeth, *Refugee Life in the Confederacy*. Baton Rouge: Louisiana State University Press, 1964.

Meade, George, *The Life and Letters of George Gordon Meade*. Vol. 1. New York: Charles Scribner's Sons, 1913.

Mercer, Philip, *The Life of the Gallant Pelham*. Macon: J. W. Burke, 1958.

Meredith, Roy, and Arthur Meredith, *Mr. Lincoln's Military Railroads*. New York: W. W. Norton, 1979.

Miles, Nelson Appleton, *Serving the Republic*. New York: Harper & Brothers, 1911.

Moore, Edward A., *The Story of a Cannoneer under Stonewall Jackson*. New York: Neale Publishing, 1907.

Myer, Albert J., *A Manual of Signals: For the Use of Signal Officers in the Field*. New York: D. Van Nostrand, 1868.

Naisawald, L. Van Loan, *The Story of the Field Artillery of the Army of the Potomac, 1861-1865*. New York: Oxford University Press, 1960.

Nisbet, James Cooper, *Four Years on the Firing Line*. Jackson, Tennessee: McCowat-Mercer, 1963.

Owen, William Miller, *In Camp and Battle with the Washington Artillery of New Orleans*. Boston: Ticknor, 1885.

Page, Charles D., *History of the Fourteenth Regiment, Connecticut Vol. Infantry*. Meriden, Connecticut: Horton, 1906.

Patrick, Marsena, *Inside Lincoln's Army: The Diary of Marsena Rudolph Patrick*. New York: Thomas Yoseloff, 1964.

Poague, William Thomas, *Gunner with Stonewall: Reminiscences of William Thomas Poague*. Jackson, Tennessee: McCowat-Mercer, 1957.

Poore, Benjamin Perley, *The Life and Public Services of Ambrose E. Burnside*. Providence: J. A. & R. A. Reid, 1882.

Pullen, John H., *The Twentieth Maine: A Volunteer Regiment in the Civil War*. Philadelphia: Lippincott, 1957.

Russell, Andrew J., *Russell's Civil War Photographs*. New York: Dover Publications, 1982.

Sanford, George B., *Fighting Rebels and Redskins*. Norman: University of Oklahoma Press, 1969.

Simpson, Harold B., *Hood's Texas Brigade: Lee's Grenadier Guard*. Dallas: Alcor Publishing, 1983.

Smith, James Power, *With Stonewall Jackson in the Army of Northern Virginia*. Gaithersburg, Maryland: Zullo and Van Sickle Books, 1982.

Stackpole, Edward J.:
Chancellorsville: Lee's Greatest Battle. Harrisburg: Stackpole, 1958.
The Fredericksburg Campaign: Drama on the Rappahannock. Harrisburg: Stackpole, 1957.

Stevens, Christian D., *Meagher of the Sword: A Dramatization of the Life of Thomas Francis Meagher*. New York: Dodd, Mead, 1967.

Stiles, Robert, *Four Years under Marse Robert*. Dayton: Morningside Bookshop, 1977.

Survivor's Association, 121st Regiment Pennsylvania Volunteers, *History of the 121st Regiment Pennsylvania Volunteers*. Philadelphia: Burk & McFetridge, 1893.

Tucker, Glenn, *Hancock the Superb*. Indianapolis: Bobbs-Merrill, 1960.

United States War Department, *The War of the Rebellion: A Compilation of the Official Records of the Union and Confederate Armies*. Series 1, Vols. 21 and 25. Washington: Government Printing Office, 1902.

Veterans of the Nineteenth Regiment Massachusetts Volunteer Infantry, *History of the Nineteenth Regiment Massachusetts Volunteer Infantry, 1861-1865*. Salem, Massachusetts: Salem Press, 1906.

Wainwright, Charles S., *A Diary of Battle*. New York: Harcourt, Brace & World, 1962.

Walker, Francis Amasa, *History of the Second Army Corps in the Army of the Potomac*. New York: Charles Scribner's Sons, 1886.

Ward, James Arthur, *That Man Haupt: A Biography of Herman Haupt*. Baton Rouge: Louisiana State University Press, 1973.

Weber, Thomas, *The Northern Railroads in the Civil War*. Westport, Connecticut: Greenwood Press, 1970.

Whan, Vorin E., Jr., *Fiasco at Fredericksburg*. State College: Pennsylvania State University Press, 1961.

Williams, Kenneth P., *Lincoln Finds a General: A Military Study of the Civil War*. Vol. 2. New York: Macmillan, 1949.

Wise, Jennings Cropper, *The Long Arm of Lee: The History of the Army of Northern Virginia*. New York: Oxford University Press, 1959.

Other sources

Bennett, Gordon C., "Grant's Railroad: Route through Danger." *Civil War Times Illustrated*, October 1983.

Bilby, Joseph G., "Remember Fontenoy!" *Military Images Magazine*, March-April 1983.

Boswell, James Keith, "The Diary of a Confederate Staff Officer." *Civil War Times Illustrated*, April 1976.

Cory, Eugene A., "A Private's Recollections of the Civil War." In Historical Society of Rhode Island, *Personal Narratives of Events in the War of the Rebellion.* 3rd Series, No. 4. Providence, 1884.

Cullen, Joseph P., "The Battle of Chancellorsville." *Civil War Times Illustrated*, May 1968.

Gladstone, William, "Sgt. Thomas Plunkett, Company E, 21st Massachusetts." *Military Images Magazine*, November-December 1984.

Keyser, Carl, "Leatherbreeches at Chancellorsville." *Civil War Times Illustrated*, August 1975.

McCarter, William, "Fredericksburg — as Seen by One of Meagher's Irish Brigade." *National Tribune*, July 29, 1886.

Mitchell, Adele, "James Keith Boswell: Jackson's Engineer." *Civil War Times Illustrated*, June 1968.

Moore, J. H., "Fredericksburg." *Confederate Bivouac*, August 1886.

Mulholland, St. Clair A., "At Fredericksburg." *National Tribune*, October 8, 1881.

Rice, Thomas, "Wading to Glory: The Misery of Burnside's Mud March." *Civil War Times Illustrated*, May 1981.

Sword, Wiley, "Cavalry on Trial at Kelly's Ford." *Civil War Times Illustrated*, April 1974.

INDEX

Time-Life Books Inc. offers a wide range of fine recordings, including a *Big Bands* series. For subscription information, call 1-800-621-7026, or write TIME-LIFE MUSIC, Time & Life Building, Chicago, Illinois 60611.